966

WEST AFRICA

*A Background Book
from Ancient Kingdoms
to Modern Times*

by James E. Trupin

with an introduction by Steven Jervis

Parents' Magazine Press · New York

Each Background Book is concerned with the broad spectrum of people, places and events affecting the national and international scene. Written simply and clearly, the books in the series will engage the minds and interests of people living in a world of great change.

For my wife, Michele, and my children, Joshua and Jessica

Acknowledgments

I WISH TO express my deepest appreciation to Mrs. Lillian McClintock for her perceptive editorial criticism and advice and to Mrs. Carole Dufrechou, Rena Friedenreich, Mrs. Natalie Goldberg, and Bridget Marmion for their invaluable assistance in the gathering of material and the preparation of this manuscript.

J. E. T.
Norwalk, Connecticut

Contents

List of Illustrations

(between pages 106 and 107)

Maps

Introduction

A DECADE OF growing global awareness, of
Black Power and the Peace Corps, has barely altered
American ignorance of Africa. We still find this
enormous continent, if not impenetrably mysterious, then cloudy and generalized, hardened into
clichés. Only a tiny percent of Americans who visit
Europe make their way south to Africa, and few who
do get beyond game parks and urban hotels. It was
nearly two hundred years before an American Secretary of State toured Africa; how much longer for a
President? The sad fact remains that, to most of us,
Africa is as dark as ever.

That darkness was dramatically evident during the
Nigerian war. Rarely has a conflict of international
moment been so little understood. Often equipped
with the finest intentions, a crowd of journalists,
writers, and alarmed citizenry arrived in the Nigerian capital, Lagos, or took the risky night flight into
Biafra. Perhaps because many of these correspond-
ents were unfamiliar with Africa, not to say Nigeria,
their reports tended to flatten the war into a melodra-
matic cartoon, complete with villains and heroes,
genocidal objectives, and unmodulated determina-
tion in the face of suffering. The ethnic complexity
of the antagonists was submerged in stereotypes, and
the divided loyalties that accompany the bitterest of
civil wars were barely suggested. It is hard to believe that Americans would have accepted so sim-

plistic a view of conflict in Europe or even, now, in Asia. The present cannot be understood without the past, but for most of us the past of Nigeria—indeed of Africa—still does not exist. A few images of spear-brandishing dancers, of mangrove swamps or of starvation: these are our easy symbols of this vast, many-peopled continent.

Such symbols are worse than inadequate; they are destructive of comprehension. We must accept the possibility that African politics, culture, history are as subtle and complicated as our own. Africa may require Western technology; it does not deserve Western condescension. Do we still need to be reminded that technology and civilization are not synonymous? Even after Nigeria and the Congo, Europe rather than Africa has been the scene of this century's worst barbarities.

Yet in working past the stale vision of "savage Africa" we should avoid a comparably pernicious distortion: to view the continent as a warm and pastoral retreat. White Americans as well as black have embraced this comforting delusion, only to discover that it can be harder to teach in Nairobi than in Harlem, that Africans are not always interested in other people's racial problems, and that daily living, from Liberia to the Congo, can be a withering struggle against entrenched bureaucracy and sloth. Americans who work and travel in Africa should be inoculated against fantasy as well as typhoid. A strong sense of realism is an essential protective agent for anyone afflicted with misleading dreams.

West Africa, the subject of this book, has a flavor

and temperament uniquely its own. Unlike East Africa, it is free from white settlement and tourism; unlike southern Africa, it has largely cast off colonial rule. The curved tropical coastline and sandy interior of West Africa can seem endlessly engrossing, dispiriting, or both, but no sober view can deny the difficulties confronting the area. Its states, all but Liberia less than a generation independent, remain by Western measurement desperately poor. Per capita income nowhere exceeds a few hundred dollars a year, and the expected funds from industrial growth are unlikely to reach the impoverised for some time—unequal distribution of wealth is a fact of West African life as well as of American. Civil corruption abounds: a passport, driver's license, a scholarship to high school or university—all have their special, unofficial price, generally extracted from those who can afford it least.

Wealth and power are accessible with almost shocking ease to the well-educated West African. We should not be surprised by the medical student who seeks only an affluent urban practice, or the Education Ph. D. who regards his degree as a quick step to political advancement. Such ambitions are no more deplorable than they are among Americans, but they are even more to be regretted, since West Africa needs devoted doctors and educators with crushing urgency. The pressures on the West African reformer are immense, as illustrated in *No Longer at Ease*, by the Nigerian novelist Chinua Achebe. The book's idealistic hero has a vision of an honest society, but sinks into the very pit of corruption from which he would rescue his countrymen. Sadly, some of West Africa's most gifted men have proved more easily corruptible than Achebe's protagonist: hence the mythical "Wabenze" tribe of newly rich Africans with Mercedes-Benz limousines.

The term "tribalism," which carries such inaccurate overtones of savagery, still articulates the deepest dilemma of the West African states: how to create a sense of nationhood from a multitude of frequently hostile ethnic groups. One of the many tragedies of the Nigerian war was the role of the intellectuals, the young men who had once been counted on to unite the country but who divided it more ruthlessly than their less Westernized forebears. Even politicians lacking ethnic feeling of their own have discovered the temptations of tribal enmity as a means toward power. All West African states are afflicted with severe economic and social ills; and, in all, tribal strife has interfered with economic and social solutions.

West Africa faces a troubled future. A decade after independence, power remains largely in the hands of the few, and in many cases the few now have guns. The Nigerian war may be the worst of its kind, but it is unlikely to be the last. The course of political liberty will be rocky, and true economic independence may prove elusive. To understand the future, whatever it may bring of hardship or triumph, we need to look at the past. This book is an aid to understanding, both in itself and as an encouragement and a temptation to further study.

—Steven Jervis, March 1971

Author's Note

SOME TIME AGO, the historian, George H. T. Kimble aptly noted that "the darkest thing about Africa has always been our ignorance of it." Few people realize that West Africa has a magnificent past, and as exciting a present, as unknown a future as Europe, the Middle East, Asia, or the Americas. It is as rich in its history as it is diverse in the many peoples who dwell in its modern cities, its tribal villages, and its desert oases. West Africa is a boundless cultural pool fed by a multitude of historical sources. The glories of the medieval empires of Ghana, Mali, and Songhai; a legacy of independence from the forest kingdoms of Ashanti and Dahomey; the Islamic revolution of Uthman dan Fodio; the sculpture of Nok and Benin; the depredations of the slave trade and the humanitarian impulse that brought Sierra Leone and Liberia into being; the nationalist response to colonialism, with its sense of pride in being both black and African—all these influences, though far apart in time, contributed in their own way to the making of what we call West Africa. But the West African story does not and will not end there for, as the Roman naturalist Pliny once wrote, there is "always something new out of Africa."

J.E.T. March 1971

The spell of Africa is upon me. This is not a country, it is a world — a universe of itself and for itself, a thing Different, Immense, Menacing, Alluring. Africa is the Spiritual Frontier of human kind.

W. E. B. DuBois

CHAPTER ONE

Kingdoms of the Western and Central Sudan

ANCIENT GHANA

The king of Ghana is a great king. In his territory are mines of gold, and under him a number of kingdoms. . . . In all this country there is gold.
— EL YAKUBI, a ninth-century chronicler[1]

THE ACTUAL FOUNDERS of the ancient state of Ghana, which lay one thousand miles to the north of the modern nation, are unknown. Some writers assert that Ghana's first rulers were North African Berbers who were eventually replaced by the black Soninke, a dynasty that governed the kingdom from the eighth century A.D. until its downfall in the thirteenth century. Other historians set Ghana's beginnings as early as the third century and say that Ghana referred to the king and meant "war chief." The king was also called *kaya maghan*, or "king of the gold." It is believed that other African kingdoms — Tekrur, Mali, and Gao — accepted the overlordship of this ruler. In any case, Ghana was the

3

name this kingdom was known by to the inhabitants of North Africa.

Much of the information upon which we base our knowledge of Ghana comes from the writings and accounts left by Arab traders and travelers who crossed the Sahara in search of markets for their goods. El Fazari, an Arab astronomer, wrote of Ghana during the eighth century as "the territory of Ghana, the land of gold."[2] Another Arab traveler, Ibn Hawqal, commented that "the kings of this city [he was speaking of Audoghast, an important trans-Saharan caravan terminal] have relations with the king of Ghana, who is the richest on earth because of his gold."[3]

Ghana's wealth and power were based on her most important resource: gold. It was mined in the district of Wangara, the central deposits being at Bambouk in the upper Senegal valley—an area just beyond Ghana's political control—and in Bouré, which is located on the upper Niger River. The Soninke people acted as traders or middlemen in the gold trades. North of Ghana and to the south of the Atlas mountain range was a town called Sijilmasa, one of the many caravan terminals where Arab and African merchants and traders met. Here, as in other market towns, the Soninke exchanged their gold, often on an even basis, for precious salt which was then used as a food preservative. In addition to salt and gold, copper, cloth, dried fruit, and cowrie shells—also used widely as a currency—were traded. In some parts of the Western Sudan today, salt, crystallized around a straw, is still sold in the market towns.

The Arab merchants then sold and traded the gold of Ghana to Europe. In fact, from the eighth century until the discovery of America and Spain's exploitation of the riches of Mexico, Peru, and the West Indies, the Western Sudan, and particularly Ghana, were Europe's main sources of gold. Because of her immense wealth, Ghana and her kings were known in the royal courts of Europe and were held in high regard there.

The capital of Ghana, which one author claims was known to its own inhabitants as Kumbi Saleh, was actually two towns lying in a plain. According to El Bakri, an Arab chronicler, one of the towns was mostly inhabited by Muslim traders. The other town, in which the king was said to have lived, contained a palace, dome-shaped houses, a mosque for visiting Muslims and diplomats, all of which were enclosed within a wall. In Europe, a wall usually marked a city in fear of outside attack, and there is every reason to believe it served the same purpose in Ghana. On the border of Mauritania, near these twin cities, archaeologists have uncovered, along with pieces of pottery and other artifacts, a city of perhaps thirty thousand inhabitants where mosques, mansions, houses, and intricate ironwork once stood.

From his court, the king of Ghana ruled an area so vast that it included all those lands within four days' ride from his capital. He organized a taxation system which consisted of placing a levy in goods or in money on products entering or leaving his kingdom. El Bakri wrote that "for every donkey loaded with salt that enters the country, the king takes a duty of one golden dinar, and two dinars from everyone that leaves."

Another tax, on gold, was collected because the king considered "all pieces of gold that are found in the empire belonged to the emperor." The king regulated the supply and trade in gold to keep its price high in order to enrich his court. A policy similar to that of the Ghanaian king's was followed by the Spanish sovereigns during Spain's Golden (sixteenth) Century when gold from the New World made her the most prosperous nation in Europe. El Bakri notes further that

> . . . the best gold found in this land comes from the town of Ghiyaru, which is eighteen days traveling from the city of the king. . . . The nuggets found in all the mines of this country are reserved for the king, only gold dust being left for the people.[4]

Another indication of the king's enormous wealth comes from the Arab chronicle, *Tarikh al-Fattash*, the oldest known historical document of the Western Sudan, which describes a Ghanaian king of the seventh century named Kanissa'ai. It was said that this ruler owned one thousand horses, each of which "slept only on a carpet, with a silken rope for a halter"[5] and each was attended by three men and treated as if each were itself a king. Unfortunately, as in many nations throughout history, the common people lived in abject poverty, were called upon to fight in Ghana's wars of conquest, and benefited little, if at all, from Ghana's gold.

The Ghanaian armies of the time were invincible, their success assured by their skillful use of iron-pointed spears. The Arab writer El Zuhri spoke of the Ghanaians battling an enemy "who knew not iron and fight with bars of ebony" and defeating them "because they [the Ghanaians] fight with swords and lances."[6] El Bakri claimed that the king of Ghana could put 200,000 men in the field of which more than 40,000 were bowmen. It was Ghanaian superiority in war, economic organization, and political skill that made this ancient nation for centuries the foremost force in the Western Sudan.

However, in the year 1040, an Islamic tribe known as the Almoravides or Marabouts swept across the Sahara. By 1054, the important caravan terminal of Audoghast, part of Ghana's vital lifeline and under her sway since 990, fell to the marauders. Ghana, once indomitable, was faced with a crisis that it would be unable to solve. Twenty-two years later, with Abu Bakr at their head, the Almoravides at last succeeded in overthrowing the Ghanaian dynasty. The conquerors immediately sought to convert the Ghanaians to Islam. While the kings of Ghana accepted Muslims as their advisers before Ghana's downfall, the king's religion and that of his followers remained pagan and many at first refused conversion. The religious tide, however, would soon turn in favor of Islam.

In 1087, Ghana was temporarily reprieved when
Abu Bakr died in battle and a greatly weakened
Soninke rule was re-established. It was to last for little over a century. With her trade routes lost and
her military superiority broken, Ghana was unable
to rekindle the flame of her past glory. In 1203, a
Fulani warrior king, Sumanguru, conquered what
is thought to be Kumbi Saleh. Ghana as an empire
was no more. Sumanguru, however, failed to bring
peace to Ghana. His disruption of the caravan routes,
a string of oppressive taxes, and the brutal nature of
his rule led to further conflict and bloodshed. In
1235, Sumanguru rode forth in battle against
Sundiata, chief of the Mandinka (or Mandingo)
people of Kangaba near the Niger's headwaters.
According to legend, an arrow was thrown from
the Mandinka ranks and, as it struck Sumanguru,
the Fulani conquerer disappeared. Kangaba eventually supplanted Ghana and, as the empire of Mali,
with Sundiata as its king, exercised political and
economic control over much of the Western Sudan.

THE EMPIRE OF MALI

"Sundiata . . . defeated the army of Sumanguru, ravaged the land of the Susu and subjugated its people. Afterwards Sundiata became the ruler of an immense empire [Mali] . . ."—an anonymous Arab writer[7]

AS GHANA DECLINED, two small rival nations arose to its east—Kaniaga and Kangaba. Kangaba, which evolved into the state of Mali, was founded by the Mandinka or Mandingo peoples in the eleventh century. During the waning years of the Ghanaian empire, the Mandingo served as middlemen in the trading centers of the Western Sudan.

Sumanguru, who had led the crushing assault on Kumbi Saleh in 1203, murdered eleven brothers of the ruling family of Kangaba. He spared but one, the crippled Sundiata Keita. His single humane act bore within it the seeds of his own downfall. In 1230, Sundiata became emperor of Kangaba and set forth to expand his own domain. In 1235, his armies defeated the rival forces of Kaniaga. Shortly after, as we have seen, Sundiata avenged the murder of his brothers when Kangaba's army crushed Sumanguru's legions, killing the Ghanaian emperor.

It is probable that Sundiata came to the throne as a pagan even though Islam had made significant headway among the people of the Western Sudan by the thirteenth century. Sundiata, however, quickly realized the advantages of conversion and became a

9

Muslim. From Sundiata's time onward, the states of
the Western Sudan would be ruled by Muslim dynasties and it was the widely traveled Muslim merchants who acted as propagators of the Islamic faith
in the Saharan cities and caravan terminals. Islam
had grown strong in the Western Sudan since its
debut two centuries before.

With the conquest of Sumanguru's Ghana, Sundiata had inherited the invaluable source of Ghana's
wealth—the Wangara mines. As a dutiful Muslim,
he set about to convert the gold miners to Islam, an
effort that nearly ended in economic disaster. As the
miners' devotion to Islam increased, gold production
declined, since more time was being spent in worship
than in mining. Finally Sundiata recognized his error
and the miners were released from their obligation
to practice the Islamic faith.

As his empire grew in size, Sundiata moved his
capital from Jeriba to Niani farther down the Niger
River. By 1240, the kingdom of Mali (which meant
"where the king resides") had become a recogniz-
able state. Sundiata ruled and conquered until 1255,
when he was succeeded by Mansa Uli, who reigned
until 1270. The two emperors extended the boundaries and increased the wealth of Mali, solidifying
their control over Mali's gold-supplying Wangara
district, subjugating Diara in the northwest, and
moving Mali's borders south along the Niger as far
as the shores of Lake Debo.

As the thirteenth century ended, Mali was the
richest and most powerful nation in the Western

Sudan, with gold mines flourishing, and Sundiata Keita was a legendary hero.

By 1307, the greatest of Mali's emperors, Mansa Musa, the grandson of Sundiata, had ascended the throne. When Mansa Musa died in 1332, Mali reigned supreme over the great trading cities of the Sahara and her influence was felt as far north as the salt deposits of Taghaza. In the east, Mali ruled over the learning centers of Timbuktu and Gao on the Niger as well as the copper mines of Takedda; in the west, she reached into gold-rich Tekrur and absorbed the gold-mining districts to the south. A European map of the time recognized the existence of the black sovereign and his magnificent kingdom: "This negro lord is called Musa Mali, Lord of the Negroes of Guinea. So abundant is the gold which is found in his country that he is the richest and most noble king in all the land."

Ibn Batuta, a North African Berber, paid a visit to Mali during Mansa Musa's reign and left this description of the ruler and his people:

> [Mansa Musa was] a generous and virtuous prince who loved the whites and made gifts to them . . . The Negroes [of Mali] possess some admirable qualities. They are seldom unjust, and have a greater abhorrence of injustice than any other people. The sultan shows no mercy to anyone who is guilty of the least act of it. There is complete security in their country. Neither traveler nor inhabitant in it has anything to fear from robbers or men of violence.[8]

Mansa Musa is perhaps most famous for his fabled

pilgrimage in 1324 to the holy city of Islam: Mecca. Before his horse marched five hundred slaves, each carrying a heavy gold staff. Behind him walked a gold-laden troop of camel. Unfortunately, Mansa Musa's generosity during his journey had its negative effect. It caused a serious slump in the Cairo gold market, which was said to have lasted for years.

Above all, Mansa Musa was a ruler conscious of the need for cultural achievements. From Mecca, he brought back to Mali the famed Andalusian poet-architect, Es-Saheli. Es-Saheli has been credited with building the great mosques of Timbuktu and Gao as well as a palace for his royal benefactor who was said to have paid him more than one thousand ounces of gold.

On his return journey, Mansa Musa took as hostage the two sons of the subject king of Songhai, in order to secure a promise of loyalty from the conquered Songhai, who lived on the banks of the middle Niger. At the time of Mansa Musa's death, the Mali empire was geographically formidable, prosperous, and its cultural institutions at Gao and Timbuktu were renowned throughout North Africa and Europe.

Mansa Musa was succeeded by his son, Maghan, whose rule was marked by strife and failure. Under Maghan, Mali's time of troubles began. From 1360 her prestige decreased as its control over its territory withered away. The Songhai hostages betrayed Maghan and returned to Gao, where one of them established himself as king of the Songhai.

Maghan's successor was, according to Ibn Batuta, Mansa Suleiman, a ruler disliked by his subjects because of his insatiable greed and cruelty. Ibn Batuta wrote that "he is a miserly king, not a man from whom one might hope for a rich present."

In 1375, Gao successfully revolted against Mandingo rule. The prized city was never recaptured. Later, from the forest lands of the south, the Mossi tribes rebelled and razed the commercial centers in Mali's Debo region. In the west, the people of Tekrur rose against their rulers. From the northeast came the raiding Taureg, capturing the important trading cities of Walata and Timbuktu en route. By the fifteenth century, the Portuguese, who had established trading enclaves on the Guinea coast, rejected Mali's appeals for assistance. No help would be forthcoming from the Europeans who were afraid of upsetting their own delicate relations with the warring nations of the Western Sudan.

So it was that the growth of new empires, economic conflicts, technical advances by rivals in metal and iron working, and a mastering by her enemies of the skills of war combined to cause Mali's downfall. By 1550 Mali was once again a minor kingdom, fragmented and virtually powerless. The seventeenth century found Mali reduced essentially to Kangaba, the area from which she had begun to expand her once-dominant empire four centuries before. As she had replaced Ghana, so too was Mali replaced by the kingdom of Songhai.

THE KINGDOM OF SONGHAI

Never has Timbuktu been profaned by the worship of idols. It is the refuge of the learned and
the devout, the habitual dwelling place of saints
and pious men. — LEO AFRICANUS, a sixteenth-
century traveler[9]

THE SONGHAI WERE a people who tilled
the fertile soil and fished the waters of the middle
Niger. In 690 A.D., the Dia or Za, a Berber tribe,
invaded peaceful Songhai. Under the Dia, Songhai's
commerce was slowly developed and expanded. The
Songhai, in 1010, adopted Islam under their ruler
Dia Kossoi. Their conversion, just as it had for Mali,
improved their economic and political relations
with Egypt and the Muslim nations of North Africa.
In fact, archaeological excavations and tombstone
writings indicate that Songhai was also in contact
with Moorish Spain. Songhai's capital, Gao, located
at the southern tip of the major trans-Saharan trade
route, became a bustling crossroads for the frequent
desert caravans.

In 1464, nearly a century after Songhai had
thrown off Mali's yoke, a remarkable black leader
emerged—the warrior-king Sunni Ali. His royal
line, the Sunni dynasty, had replaced the Dia rulers
in 1335. Also known as Ali Ber and the Si, Sunni
Ali engaged and defeated Songhai's many enemies.
Timbuktu, which had fallen to the Muslim Taureg
in 1433, buckled before the Si's onslaught in Janu-

ary 1468. Sunni Ali was a nominal Muslim himself and used the trappings of the faith, such as accepting the oath of conformity to Islam, to rally support for his cause within the Muslim community. Yet the revenge he wreaked upon those Muslims in Timbuktu whom he suspected of collaborating with the Taureg, or who declined to give him their unflinching support, was swift and often brutal. Following his victory, Sunni Ali began a bloody purge of Muslim scholars. By 1470 it was said that not a scholar could be found in Timbuktu who could write in the Arabic script.

Muslim historians have undoubtedly exaggerated the degree of Sunni Ali's vengeance. It must be remembered, though, that as a black African he probably considered the influence of Islam a threat to his purely African world.

Sunni Ali was a witch doctor who was believed by his subjects to have supernatural powers. Tradition claims for him the power to use magic charms which enabled his soldiers and their horses to fly, or to make themselves invisible, or to change themselves into serpents. Ancient tales tell of Sunni Ali's alliance with vultures, and of his ability to transform his horse, Zinzinbadio, into a vulture. One old motto presents the following picture of him:

Si [Sunni Ali] flies in the night
Si flies at first cockcrow
Si takes all the souls
Si kills the man between the hair and the head
Si kills the man between the shoe and the foot
Si kills the man between the jacket and the neck[10]

Sunni Ali was a military and political genius whose twenty-eight-year rule was marked by an unbroken string of victories. In 1473, five years after his Timbuktu triumph, the Saharan city of Jenné, known both for its gold market and for kola nuts imported from the southern forest lands, was brought within Sunni Ali's orbit. By 1476, the lake region west of Timbuktu on the middle Niger was incorporated into the Songhai kingdom. Sunni Ali fought and defeated the Mossi and the Fulani, each in their own turn.

But, from the 1480s, Songhai was to be shaken by revolts and Sunni Ali was called upon to suppress them. During an invasion by the Mossi in November 1492, the year in which the Moors and the Jews were being expelled from Spain, and the year in which Christopher Columbus sailed to the Western Hemisphere, Sunni Ali drowned under mysterious circumstances, his body later disappearing into the bush.

Sunni Ali, conquerer, politician, and witch doctor, left his people a marvelous legacy. As an African king, he had succeeded, where many others had failed, in weakening foreign influences. His Songhai was an African nation, a black kingdom that absorbed and Africanized the faith of Islam.

Sunni Ali was followed on the throne by his son, Sunni Baru, who proved, as so often happens, a terrible disappointment. Fourteen months after the death of his father, Sunni Baru was deposed by a rebellious court official, Muhammad Touré of Tekrur. Muhammad Touré or Askia Muhammad, was destined to become the greatest of Songhai's black kings.

Leo Africanus, a Spanish-born Moor, visited Askia Muhammad's court and was duly impressed:

> The rich king of Timbuktu hath many plates and scep-
> tres of gold . . . and he keeps a magnificent and well-
> furnished court. When he travelleth any whither he rideth
> upon a camel which is led by some of his noblemen; and
> so he doth likewise when he goeth forth to warfare, and
> all his soldiers ride upon horses.[11]

Askia Muhammad sought first to eliminate the deep-seated frictions caused by the Sunni family and concentrated on winning the support of the heavily Muslim towns. He was an effective administrator who divided his empire into provinces, each with its own governor, a system similar to the one used by the ancient Persians. Ministries to handle the many problems of justice, agriculture, and finance were created and each town had its own tax collector. The army was now recruited from among the slaves and war prisoners rather than being raised from the Songhai themselves. Songhai's economy soon revived because the new draft policy freed the farmers to cultivate their land and the merchants to carry on with their trade.

Timbuktu, under Askia the Great, once more became the foremost center of learning in the Western Sudan and courses in theology, Islamic law, rhetoric, grammar, and literature were taught at its university. Visiting lecturers from the North African intellectual communities of Fez and Cairo flocked to Timbuktu. It was here, too, that the black historian Mahmout Kati began to write the classic *Tarikh al-Fattash.*

Leo Africanus saw in Timbuktu: "a great store of doctors, judges, priests, and other learned men, that are bountifully maintained at the king's cost and charges and hither [to Timbuktu] are brought written books out of Barbary [North Africa], which are sold for more money than any other merchandise."[12]

As a warrior, Askia the Great extended Songhai's borders in all directions. At the peak of his power, Askia Muhammad's kingdom stretched north to the Saharan salt mines and the borders of Morocco, northeast to the towns of Air and the ancient market of Agades (around which the king settled Songhai colonists and where their descendants are still found today; east to Kano, and to the Atlantic in the west.

Inspired by the splendor of Mansa Musa's pilgrimage nearly two centuries before, Askia Muhammad journeyed to Mecca in 1495 – 1497. The treasure he brought with him, reported at 1,250 ounces of gold, rivaled Mansa Musa's and his visit cemented Songhai's relations with the world of Islam. For his efforts, Askia Muhammad was honored with the Caliphate of Tekrur (Western Sudan) by the Sherif of Mecca.

In 1528, Askia Muhammad's long reign was over. Blind, and more than eighty years old, he was deposed by his son, Askia Musa.

Unfortunately, Askia Muhammad's political talents were not inherited by his successors and Songhai went into a rapid decline. On the coast, the Portuguese had ensconced themselves at Elmina on the Gold Coast, and gold from Bouré and Bambouk, which had previously crossed the Sahara toward Morocco and North Africa, now traveled west to the Atlantic. The ensuing loss to Songhai and the rulers of the Mahgreb was enormous. Songhai's problems were compounded when the sultan of Morocco, Ahmed el-Mansur, began to cast envious eyes upon the salt mines of the Sahara. Ahmed el-Mansur's first order of business, however, was to rid himself of the growing European menace. In 1578, he decisively defeated the Portuguese at Al-Ksar. With the Portuguese temporarily eliminated, El Mansur turned his attention toward Songhai. On October 29, 1590, a Moroccan army, commanded by the Spanish Muslim Judar Pasha, and numbering 4,000 troops supplied by 9,000 pack animals, departed from Marrakech in Morocco. The Songhai king, Askia Ishak, aware of the approaching invaders, dispatched 27,000 troops to meet the Moroccans at Tondibi, near Gao, on the Niger. On April 12, 1591, Judar's army, though reduced by disease to one thousand armed soldiers and cavalry, managed to rout the numerically superior Songhai forces.

The Western Sudan's largest empire crumbled along with its army. By 1618, Songhai's economy had been ruined, Timbuktu had been pillaged, and anarchy reigned throughout the once-proud black kingdom.

KANEM-BORNU

Now as for the Blacks who went westwards toward the Mahgreb, they have divided the country, so that they now have a number of Kingdoms. The first of their Kingdoms is that of the
Zaghawa, and they inhabit the territory which is
called Kanem. — AL YAKUBI, a ninth-century
Arab chronicler[13]

THERE ARE MANY theories concerning the
origin of the Kanem kingdom, the nucleus of the
Kanem-Bornu empire. The most probable of these
hypotheses suggests that by 800 A.D., the So, Kanuri,
and Zaghawa tribes from the north, among others,
infiltrated and settled in the Lake Chad region to
the southeast of Songhai. In Kanem's early years its
population is believed to have been an aggregate of
black and white peoples. Because it lay directly in
the path of the trans-Saharan caravans, Kanem became a commercial crossroads through which West
Africa's wares were exchanged for the products of
North Africa.

Eventually, the Kanuri became the dominant tribe
in Kanem. It was from the Kanuri that the durable
Sefuwa dynasty emerged, a royal line which would
rule Kanem and them Bornu for nearly a thousand
years. The Sefuwa king traditionally selected his
bride from among the lighter-skinned Saharan aristo-
cracy. Not until the thirteenth century was a black
king thought to have reigned over Kanem's people

Cattle raising and agricultural pursuits remained

20

the main occupation of Kanem's tribesmen, but as early as the tenth century Kanem experienced a marked rise in the growth of her towns. Along with this trend toward urbanization, political authority was also becoming more centralized. A thirteenth-century geographer, Yakut, using a tenth-century eyewitness account, reported that "their [the Kanuri] houses are all of gypsum, and also the castle of their king. They respect and worship him to the neglect of Allah the most High; . . . He has absolute power over his subjects, and appropriates what he will of their belongings. Their cattle are goats and cows and camels and horses."[14]

In the eleventh and twelfth centuries, the Sefuwa king was advised by a grand council composed of twelve members and, from the available evidence, the monarchy appears to have been an almost elective office. During the late eleventh century, Islam made inroads in Kanem as it had in Mali and Songhai when the Kanuri king, Mai Umme Jilmi (later Ibn Abd el-Jehl) adopted the religion.

As Kanem grew in strength, Dunama I (1097–1150), Umme's son, expanded his empire northward, but it was not until the thirteenth century that the greater part of the Lake Chad basin fell under Kanem's banner. Its sudden elevation to a position of importance in the Central Sudan was recognized throughout North Africa. The medieval Arab historian, Ibn Khaldun, relates the excitement caused by the arrival of Kanem's envoys to the Tunisian court in 1257:

The Sultan el-Mustansir received a rich present from one of the Kings of the Negroes, the sovereign of Kanem and lord of Bornu, a town situated on the meridian of Tripoli. Among the gifts which this Negro delegation presented to him was a giraffe. . . . The inhabitants of Tunis ran in a crowd to see it, to such an extent that the plain was choked with people.[15]

Success in commerce and warfare was no guarantee against internal strife and intrigue, however. Coupled with the frequent raids by the Bulala tribe from the east, Kanem's monarchy soon found itself tottering on the brink of collapse. In 1386, the Bulala finally overran Kanem, and the defeated *mai*, or king, Omar, fled westward with his court to the neighboring province of Bornu.

Leo Africanus saw Bornu as a

. . . large province, the situation of [which] is very uneven, some part thereof being mountainous, and the residue plaine. Upon the plaines are sundry villages inhabited by rich merchants, and abounding with corne. The king of this kingdome and all his followers dwell in a certaine large village. The mountaines being inhabited by herdsmen and shepherds do bring forth mill and other graine altogether unknowen to us.[16]

Leo wrote, too, of the continuous warfare:

[The king] is at perpetuall enmitie with a certaine people inhabiting beyond the desert of Seu [Sahara]; who in times past marching with an huge armie of footmen over the saide desert, wasted a great part of the kingdome of Borno . . . [On this occasion] the King returned home conqueror with a great number of captives.[17]

Once the Sefuwa line reestablished itself in Bornu, its rule changed drastically. It became more despotic and less responsive to its subjects than it had been in Kanem. The Sefuwa dynasty may have abandoned Kanem, but it imported all of its problems and weaknesses into Bornu. As a result, the new nation was in a state of upheaval for nearly a century. It was only after the accession of Ali Ghaji (1476–1507), a ruler of the stature of Sunni Ali, that order was restored to turbulent Bornu.

At Ali Ghaji's death, the fortunes of the beleaguered Sefuwa dynasty took a turn for the better. Bornu had become powerful enough to undertake a campaign against the Bulala in whose grip Kanem remained. Idris Katakarmabe, or Idris II, (1507–1529) mounted an army and headed east. A fierce battle with the Bulala ensued and Njimi, Kanem's capital, fell to the invaders. The Sefuwa dynasty had at last retrieved their ancestral land, which had been lost to the Bulala more than a century before.

While Bornu had prospered under the Sefuwa kings, Bulala-ruled Kanem had regressed. Idris II had little difficulty in reducing Kanem to a protectorate, permitting the Bulala to reign, yet requiring of them the annual payment of tribute. While the Bulala grudgingly recognized the Sefuwa dynasty as its overlord, they anxiously awaited an opportunity to strike back in revenge. Their chance came under Bornu's next *mai*, Muhammad (1529–44). Unfortunately for the Bulala, they could not muster the strength to break the Sefuwa hold. Though they were defeated once more, the Bulala remained an unsettling element in Kanem-Bornu's midst.

When Mai Ali (1544–1548), became king of Kanem-Bornu, he found his empire pitted against the armies of the belligerent young state of Kebbi to the west. The dispute was over the division of spoils acquired during a joint campaign. Ali seemed assured of victory when, without warning, he inexplicably retreated with the Kebbi army in hot pursuit. It was only the intervention of Katsina, a Hausa nation, chafing under Kebbi's sovereignty, that saved Kanem-Bornu from an embarrassing defeat

A series of revolts during the sixteenth century rattled Bornu to its foundations, yet she managed to survive and rise to even greater heights, particularly under the guidance of her most talented and brilliant *mai*, Idris Alooma. The son of Mai Ali and a Bulala mother, Idris Alooma was raised in Kanem. The target of many an assassination plot, he barely survived childhood. His royal apprenticeship had been a harrowing experience, which left a deep impression on him. When he came to Bornu's throne in 1580, Idris Alooma was well versed in the dangers involved in heading so volatile a nation as Bornu. He was a man of extraordinary perception and intelligence, and the innovations that occurred during his rule revolutionized Bornu. From Turkey, he imported arms and military advisers. Ibn Fartua, a contemporary observer, recorded a meeting between the Turkish sultan's messengers and Idris Alooma:

On the next day all mounted after arraying themselves and their horses in armor, cuirasses, shields, and their best apparel. When we had proceeded a short distance towards the west we met messengers of the king, the Lord of Stambul, the Sultan of Turkey, who had been sent to our Sultan. . . . O my wise friends and companions! Have you ever seen a king equal to our Sultan [Idris Alooma] or like him at the time when the Lord of Stambul, the Sultan of Turkey, sent messengers to him from his country with favorable proposals.[18]

Skilled in diplomacy, Idris Alooma also had an enviable string of military successes. Unlike Songhai's military genius, Sunni Ali, Idris Alooma attracted support by basing his power on the Islamic faith. It was used to justify his policies, one of which was the further personalization of his rule. When Idris Alooma died in 1617, Kanem-Bornu had been raised to the peak of its power.

A period of relative peace prevailed for a time after Idris Alooma's death, but Kanem-Bornu could not sustain the greatness brought to it by him. When another Mai Ali became king in 1657, slowly, but with ominous certainty, Kanem-Bornu's empire began to split apart. Under the succeeding *mais*, she was faced by an assortment of enemies on her northern and southern frontiers. As the eighteenth century came to a close, she suffered another blow when a devastating famine wracked the weakened kingdom.

Uthman dan Fodio's Islamic revolution, which took place in the early nineteenth century, spared

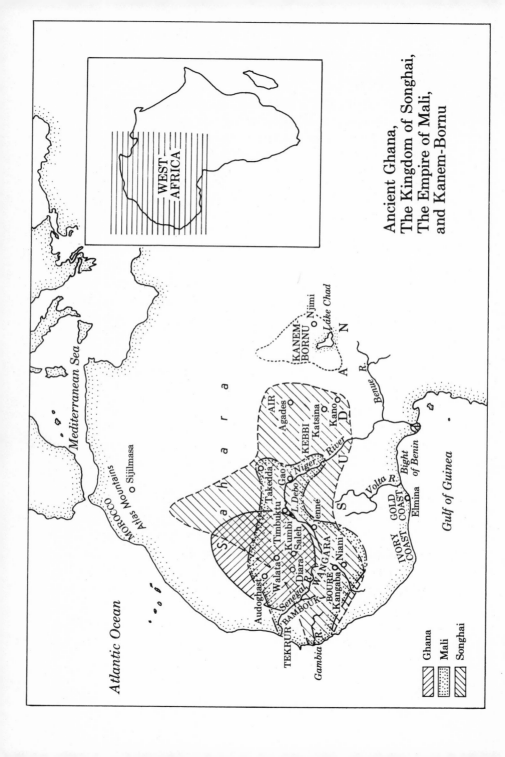

Ancient Ghana,
The Kingdom of Songhai,
The Empire of Mali,
and Kanem-Bornu

few nations in West Africa. (See the section on the
Fulani.) Kanem-Bornu was no exception. She suffered from frequent raids by the Bagirmi and Wadai
allies of the puritanical Muslim reformer and warrior. The armies of these states easily defeated Kanem and set their sights on Bornu. The initial assaults against her failed but Mai Ahmad, who
reigned from 1793 to 1810, foreseeing disaster if he
sought to confront the raiders alone, requested and
received assistance from the Kanembu people. El-
Kanemi, the Kanembu leader, a major figure in
Uthman's Fulani revolution and the ruler who
ultimately revived Bornu's fortunes, deposed the
trusting Ahmad in 1810. El-Kanemi's court was
visited in the 1820s by the English explorers,
Captain Hugh Clapperton, Major Dixon Denham,
and Dr. Walter Oudney:

> Soon after daylight, we were summoned to attend the
> Sultan of Bornu. He received us in an open space in
> front of the royal residence. We were kept at a consider-
> able distance while his people approached to within about
> 100 yards, passing first on horse-back; and after dis-
> mounting and prostrating themselves before him, they
> took their places on the ground in front, but with their
> backs to the royal person, which is the custom of the
> country. He was seated in a sort of cage of cane or wood,
> near the door of his garden, on a seat which . . . appeared
> to be covered with silk or satin, and through the railing
> looked upon the assembly before him, who formed a sort
> of semi-circle extending from his seat to nearly where we
> were waiting.[19]

El-Kanemi's reign was cut short by his death in

1835. His son, Umar, succeeded him. In 1846, Ibrahim, the last Sefuwa *mai*, rebelled against Umar and,
with the mercenary army of the Sultan of Wadai at
his command, invaded Bornu. During the course of
this uprising, Ibrahim was executed. His death sig-
naled the end of the enfeebled Sefuwa dynasty.

Bornu's remarkable recovery under El-Kanemi
and Umar did not survive the century. She was soon
faced with her most formidable adversary—the European imperialists. Piece by piece, the Bornu sultanate was dismantled and, in 1893, her throne was
usurped for a brief time by Rabeh, an adventurer
from the eastern Sudan. Rabeh proved to be no
match for the Europeans. In 1900, his cavalry
clashed with a French column and was soundly defeated. During the skirmish, Rabeh died. The
French claim to Bornu, however, was contested by
the British and the Germans. Finally, by 1906, an
agreement between the powers was reached. The
once-vast Bornu kingdom was divided among the
British, French, and German colonial empires.

CHAPTER TWO

The Forest, the Rivers, and the Sea

THE MOSSI NATIONS

The Mossi empires . . . have at all times constituted an impregnable rampart against the extension of Islamism, which has never had any hold
on them. Although counting among their subjects a certain number of Mussulmans all of
whom were foreigners, . . . they have remained
profoundly attached to the old local religion and
rightly pass as representing, in all its integrity, a
civilization which is uniquely and really Negro. — MAURICE DELAFOSSE in *The Negroes of Africa*, 1931.[20]

IT IS SAID that a prince named Widiraogo, a
son of a Malinke king, set forth from the place
where the Black and White Volta rivers converge
and flow toward the sea and conquered his neighbors, after which he established a kingdom he called
Dagomba. Widiraogo's dates are unknown, but he is
believed to have died in the early eleventh century.
His empire was split into three more or less equal

parts. Widiraogo's first son, Zungurana, was given
the western region; the second son, Rau, inherited
the northwestern territories around Diara; and the
third son, Diaba-Lompo, was willed the eastern possessions.

Zungurana's son, Ubri, is supposed to have founded Wagadugu in 1050, and then annexed other
lands. This root nation was to grow into the empire
which was called Mossi after its inhabitants. Rau's
grandson and uncle consolidated Yatenga and
Diaba-Lompo's state to form the nucleus of Gurma.
Eventually, five principal Mossi nations emerged—
Wagadugu (Ougadougou), Yatenga, Fada-n-Gurma,
Mamprussi, and Dagomba. Each of these states became a power in its own right and remained, for the
most part, independent for over eight hundred
years. They were located where the modern West
African nations of Upper Volta and Ghana are now.

Because they were on the fringes of the Western
Sudan, the Mossi states were constantly subjected to
attacks by the armies of Mali and Songhai from the
eleventh century onward and by the Ashanti in the
eighteenth century. They successfully withstood the
Mali and Songhai invasions. In fact, an avenging
army led by the *naba*, or king, of Yatenga turned the
tables on Mali and invaded and sacked Timbuktu in
1333. The Mossi became a constant source of fear
and irritation to the larger nations of the Western
Sudan. Even after Sunni Ali drove them off in the
fifteenth century, they continued to harass Songhai
and her vassal states.

War, however, did not preoccupy the Mossi. While they undertook occasional campaigns against their rivals, they much preferred to serve as intermediaries in the trading posts along West Africa's caravan routes.

The Mossi administrative system resembled those of the other nations of the Western Sudan. They were ruled by a monarch, the *morho-naba*, who was assisted in his decision-making by a council of eleven ministers, only one of whom was a Muslim. The council exercised the usual powers of taxation, justice, and the administering of the empire, all under the watchful eye of the *morho-naba*. The Mossi kingdom was divided into provinces, cantons, and villages with each state accepting and recognizing the *morho-naba's* supreme authority.

Unlike Mali and Songhai, the Mossi peoples succeeded in resisting the pressures of Islamic conversion and, until their conquest by the French in the late nineteenth century, practiced their traditional religions. Like the Songhai, the Mossi states were distinctly black African nations, bound to their own, rather than to imported, religious traditions.

As an example of political stability, the Mossi were second to none in the history of the Western Sudan. Their love of independence and their fierce desire to preserve it were only subdued when the Ashanti (see page 53) reduced Mamprussi and Dagomba to tributaries in the mid-eighteenth century and the French, in 1896, declared a protectorate over the Mossi empire.

THE HAUSA STATES

Kano had been sounding in my ears for more than a year; it had been one of the great objects of our journey as the central point of commerce, as a great storehouse of information, and as the point whence more distant regions might be most successfully attempted. At length, after nearly a year's exertions, I had reached it. — HEINRICH BARTH, a European explorer, in 1851[21]

THE SIX ORIGINAL Hausa nations were located in the north of modern Nigeria. According to the popular legend of Daura, the tenth-century ancestor of the Hausa rulers, Abuyazidu, married the Queen of Daura, who, in time, bore him a son. This prince, Bawo, fathered six sons, each of whom ruled a Hausa state: "Gazaura who became king of Daura, Bagauda who became king of Kano, Gunguma who became king of Zazzau [Zaria], Duma who became king of Gobir, Kumayau who became king of Katsina, and Zamna Kogi who became king of Rano."[22] Other West African myths include Biram among the early Hausa states.

These monarchs reigned over relatively small kingdoms, each of which contained a walled capital, since warfare was common in tenth-century Hausaland.

The Hausa states varied in size and importance. Rano remained a minor settlement while Kano blossomed into a thriving commercial and cultural center. Daura, in northeast Hausaland, survived, but her sister state, Biram, was eventually swallowed up during the expansion of Bornu. Zazzau or Zaria, Gobir, and Katsina at one time or another during the next eight centuries took turns in dominating Hausaland.

Archaeological evidence indicates that Kano was first settled by Berbers migrating westward across the Sahara. Her first *sarki*, or king, ascended the throne in 999. Kano's renown spread quickly beyond the confines of the Sahara, and Leo Africanus, who stopped there in 1510, took note of the Hausa nation:

> The great province of [Kano] standeth eastward of the river Niger almost five hundred miles. The greatest part of the inhabitants dwelling in villages are some of them herdsmen and others husbandmen. Here groweth abundance of corn, of rice, and of cotton. . . . In the midst of this province standeth a towne called by the same name, the walles and houses whereof are built of a kind of chalke. The inhabitants are rich merchants and most civill people. Their king was in times past of great [power], and had mighty troupes of horsemen at his command.[23]

Kano and the other Hausa kingdoms, through their trade and resources, became economically self-sufficient. The Hausa kingdoms' many merchants embraced Islam and used Arabic script despite the reluctance of their rulers to follow suit. In fact, while Islam permeated Hausaland, its influence on the Hausa monarchies was uneven and remained so until the nineteenth-century Fulani revolution. During the fourteenth century, the fascinating *Kano Chronicle* remarked that Kano's *sarki*, Garazawa, "was opposed to prayer, and when the Muslims, after praying, had gone home, he would come with his men and defile the whole mosque and cover it with filth."[24] The grip of tradition proved hard to break.

From its creation, Kano was outward-looking. Under Sarki Muhammad Rumfa (1465-1499), Kano improved its political relations with Songhai and Kanem-Bornu. These contacts greatly affected her subsequent development. Kano's government was centralized and when Songhai, with whom she sometimes clashed, fell before the invading Moroccan armies in the sixteenth century, her economy benefited greatly. Timbuktu and Jenné could no longer compete with Kano and her far-ranging and ambitious traders. Her merchants moved into areas where the Mande (Mandingo) merchants once held undisputed sway. Cotton was Kano's major export and the basis of her wealth and power. As late as the mid-nineteenth century, Heinrich Barth commented on Kano's still active role as the supplier of cotton cloth to West Africa:

> The great advantage of Kano is that commerce and manufactures go hand in hand, and that almost every family has its share in them. There is really something grand in this kind of industry which spreads to the north as far as . . . Tripoli; to the west, not only to Timbuktu, but in some degree even as far as the shores of the Atlantic. . . .[25]

In the sixteenth century, however, the signs of

Kano's decline were already evident. Her economy depended upon the use of slave labor and it was the unending quest for slaves which led to self-destructive wars. These conflicts sapped her strength and eventually proved to be her undoing. Kano and her Hausa neighbors, who also engaged in slave trading, all passed, at one time or another, into the control of other, stronger West African empires.

During the sixteenth century, the Hausa nations had to contend with the Kebbi nation to the west. Kebbi's taste for conflict and pillage, rather than steady economic progress, was behind her meteoric rise. Muhammad Bello, the nineteenth-century Muslim scholar, son of Uthman dan Fodio and Sultan of Sokoto (in northern Nigeria), within whose sultanate Kebbi lay, described the city-state and its history:

> [Kebbi was] extensive and well-watered and had many trees and sand. The kingdom dates from the time of Kanta [king]. It is said that Kanta was a slave of the Fulani. He rose up and conquered towns and ruled countries far and near. It is even said that his rule extended over Katsina and Kano and Gobir and Zazzau [Zaria] and the town of Air and half the land of Songhai. He also made war on Bornu. . . . No other kingdom in the past history of these countries ever equalled it in power.[26]

As Bello indicated, Kebbi subjugated many of her Hausa rivals, and as we have already seen, she did not shrink from confrontations with larger nations such as Songhai and Bornu.

Kebbi's hegemony over Hausaland lasted until the Hausa king of Gobir, with the assistance of soldiers from Air and Zamfara, combined to crush Kebbi's cavalry and destroy her garrison towns of Ghunghu, Surame, and Lika. The ruins of Surame are still visible today to the west of Sokoto. Muhammad Bello remarked that "though it is about a hundred years since [Kebbi's] cities were broken, [they] surpass any we have ever seen."

In Leo Africanus' time, Katsina was not as impressive to the Moorish scholar as the other Hausa nations he visited:

> Casena [Katsina], bordering eastward upon [Kano], is full of mountains and drie flelds, which yield not withstanding great store of barlie and millfeed. The inhabitants are all extremely black [and] they dwell in most forlorne and base cottages; neither shall you find any of their villages above three hundred families.[27]

Yet, in the nineteenth century, Heinrich Barth could recount, in his book, *Travels and Discoveries in North and Central Africa*, that:

> The town [Katsina], if only half its immense area were ever tolerably well inhabited, must certainly have had a population of at least a hundred thousand souls. . . . In fact, Katsina, during the seventeenth and eighteenth centuries . . . seems to have been the chief city of this part of Negroland, as well in commercial and political importance as in other respects.[28]

Zaria, too, dominated part of Hausaland during the sixteenth century. Like Kano, Katsina, and Kebbi, she trafficked in slaves. But Zaria was unique in another respect. She had a royal line of politically able and wise female rulers whose diplomatic skills gained for her a key position in the trans-Saharan caravan trade.

By the eighteenth century, when Gobir and Katsina were ascendant and the Europeans clamored for slaves, Hausaland had become a major slave-hunting ground. After 1750, Hausaland's fortunes dipped badly. Taureg raiders from the north threatened her frontiers. Within Hausaland itself, the Fulani-led economic and religious revolution—which had its roots in Gobir—was spreading quickly. Embattled on her borders and plagued by internal disorders, Hausaland drifted toward collapse. In the first decade of the nineteenth century, the armies of the Muslim preacher-revolutionary, Uthman dan Fodio, conquered most of Hausaland. For the first time in their history, unity was imposed upon the Hausa nations by their Muslim conquerors as Hausaland was incorporated into the huge Fulani empire.

IFE, OYO, AND THE YORUBA KINGDOMS

The country of Yoruba is extensive and has streams and rocks and hills. There are many curious and beautiful things in it. The ships of Christians come there . . . In the land of Yoruba are found birds green in colour which are called "babgha" in Arabic and we call "Aku" [a parrot]. It is a bird which talks and is beautiful.
—MUHAMMAD BELLO[29]

CENTURIES BEFORE THE birth of Christ, the Nok civilization was flourishing in central Nigeria north of the Niger-Benue confluence. The most outstanding aspect of this culture was its sculpture—life-size figures rendered in terra cotta. What is remarkable about this art form is the high degree of technical skill required for its creation. It is all the more impressive an achievement when one realizes that Nok's neighbors had only the most rudimentary tools at their command. Many mysteries still surround Nok daily life and it is unlikely that much new information will be uncovered in the near future. Fortunately, though the Nok civilization itself disappeared, its artistic refinements survived and next appeared in Ife, the Yoruba spiritual center, almost a thousand years later.

The Yoruba peoples comprise one of the largest of Nigeria's tribal groupings. They are also found in Dahomey and Togo. There has been much conjec-

ture over their origins. The Yoruba are thought to
have descended from the Berbers who migrated to
Nigeria before 1000 A.D. One theory has two migra-
tory streams entering the region, one headed toward
Ife and the other moving in the direction of Oyo
above the steaming rain forest. Research still continues and Yoruba origins have yet to be definitely
determined.

In Yorubaland, whose topography ranges from
forest to lagoon and wooded savannah, there is
much overlap in oral tradition. In Oyo, as well as in
Benin and the other states that sprang up in the area,
tales frequently tell of a common past.

Their origin is attributed by the Yoruba themselves to Olorun, or God, who instructed his son,
Oduduwa, to create the earth. Oduduwa, being a
dutiful son, founded Ife, which became the Mecca,
or Jerusalem, of the Yoruba. His work completed,
Oduduwa was said to have married a sea goddess,
and the children born of this marriage became the
founders of the many Yoruba settlements that spotted West Africa.

Another popular version of the Yoruba myth has
Oduduwa breaking faith with Islam and turning to
pagan idol worship. For this transgression, Oduduwa
was expelled from Mecca and, with his disciples,
crossed Africa and settled in Ife. Upon reaching Ife,
Oduduwa married. His wife gave birth to seven children, each of whom were ancestors of the monarchs
who later ruled the Yoruba nations of Ila, Ketu,
Oyo, Owu, Popo, Sabe, and Benin. The Hausa, too,

speak of seven offspring, Berber in ancestry, who
came to rule their kingdoms.

Samuel Johnson, an English missionary in nineteenth-century Oyo, recounts another variation
of the Oduduwa legend:

> Yorubas are said to have sprung from Lamdurudu, one
> of the kings of Mecca, whose offspring were . . . Odudu-
> wa, the ancestor of the Yorubas, the Kings of Gogobiri
> and of the Kukawa, two tribes in the Hausa country.

Johnson also notes the common physical makeup
of the Hausa and Yoruba:

> These two nations, notwithstanding the lapse of time
> since their separation and in spite of the distance from
> each other, . . . still have the same distinctive tribal
> marks on their faces; and Yoruba travellers are free
> amongst them and vice versa, each recognising each other
> as of one blood.[30]

The town of Ife, despite its supreme spiritual role,
was prevented, because of its inaccessible location,
from becoming a commercial center of any signifi-
cance. As a cultural center, however, it was famous
for its bronze and terra cotta sculpture. These usually took the form of female and male busts and are
believed to have been used as burial monuments.
Many art historians have found a likeness between
Ife and Greek and Renaissance sculpture. However,
as with Nok, it has not been established whether the
art of Ife evolved independently or resulted from
Mediterranean influences. Perhaps the reverse could
be the case, with the techniques of Nok and Ife

moving northward and beyond the Mediterranean.

Ife's religious leader was called the *Oni*. All the Yoruba rulers sought his sanction, for without it their rule might be considered illegitimate. Even the powerful *alafins*, or kings, of Oyo paid homage to the *Oni*.

Oyo lay to the northwest of Ife, beyond the rain forest. Its position was important commercially because a number of trade routes passed through Oyo with the products of West Africa and the Sahara. It is thought that Oyo was a strategic creation, founded as a brace against the threatening kingdoms of Nupe and Borgu to the northwest.

Tradition credits the god Oranmiyan with Oyo's establishment. His work completed, he became Oyo's first *alafin*. This was believed to have taken place at the end of the fourteenth century. The *alafin*, rather than being a divinity unto himself, was considered more a consort of the Yoruba gods. When an *alafin* died (his son was forbidden to succeed him) an elaborate system came into operation whereby the *oyo mesi*, who were originally seven Chief Councillors of State, would elect a new *alafin*. The concentration of power within one family and therefore the chances for tyranny were thus theoretically limited to the *alafin's* lifetime. The *oyo mesi* also had the authority to condemn an inept *alafin* to death.

By the middle of the sixteenth century, what Oyo had feared for two centuries came to pass. The armies of the Nupe empire drove the *alafin* from Oyo.

His flight ended in Borgu where he was given refuge. For Nupe, the victory proved a mixed blessing,
for it was in Borgu that Oyo's military was reorgan-
ized and, with horses imported from North Africa, a
cavalry was mounted and Oyo was retaken. While it
met with great success in its northern sorties, the
fearsome Oyo cavalry proved more of a hindrance in
the southern forest terrain. However, by circling the
forest, Oyo did manage to acquire a considerable
stretch of territory. By the end of the seventeenth
century, Dahomey and the Atlantic slave trade out-
lets of Porto Novo and Whydah had been taken by
Oyo's mobile army. In southwestern Nigeria, as the
eighteenth century opened, Oyo reigned supreme,
her empire at its apex.

It was a situation too good to last. In the 1720s, it
was evident that Oyo had overextended herself. To
the west, the emerging kingdom of Dahomey challenged Oyo's hegemony by invading her satellite,
Allada. In response, Oyo struck at Dahomey repeatedly until, by 1750, the young nation was reduced to
an Oyo tributary. The Dahomean campaigns and her
own deep involvement in the slave trade began to
exact their toll on Oyo. Her economy was suffering
and her government was tangled in a web of in-
trigues. In 1754, shortly after the end of the Dahomean conflict, Gaha, the *basorun* or chief minister,
usurped the *alafin's* throne. His ruthlessness caused
a popular uprising and he was overthrown in 1774.

When the deposed *alafin*, Abiodun, was finally
restored to power, Oyo was a changed society. Dur-

ing Gaha's rule, Oyo experienced a decline as Yorubaland's great power. She again clashed with Dahomey, which sought to cast off her tributary status.
While it remained under Oyo's suzerainty until
1822, Dahomey's unrelenting assaults against her
and her coastal possessions (especially those engaged in the slave trade), further drained Oyo's waning strength. Both Borgu and Nupe inflicted crushing defeats on the *alafin's* cavalry and, in 1796, the
Egba peoples to the south rebelled. Clearly, Oyo
had become a shadow of her former self. Within her
domain, revolts spread like an epidemic as other
tributaries began to assert themselves.

The nineteenth century held out little hope for
Oyo's revival. Her slave trading ports were blockaded by the British navy after 1808. The Fulani
jihads were in full swing, threatening any nation that
lay in their path. Dahomey and Ilorin, the city-state
to the south of Oyo, had both gained their independence. By the 1820s, Oyo's empire had been
peeled away to a small core.

In an effort to salvage a small part of his shrinking
kingdom, Oyo's last *alafin*, Aluewu, moved against
Ilorin in 1837, but treachery within his own ranks
caused his defeat. After the battle, during which the
alafin was killed, Oyo itself was abandoned. Those
who survived the catastrophe trekked southward and
founded New Oyo, near the Yoruba town of Ibadan,
upon whose armies they could depend for protection. The thriving settlement of Ibadan served its purpose, turning back Fulani onslaughts until the dan-

ger of invasion abated in the mid-1840s. The faded glory of Old Oyo, the axis upon which the Yoruba nations once revolved, was never recaptured. In 1887, the independence of Oyo, old and new, passed into history as the British resident in Lagos persuaded the reigning *alafin* to submit to British "protection." Within five years, Ibadan and Abeokuta, to the south, the stronghold of the Egba peoples, were also swallowed up by the British advance inland.

BENIN

The country of Benin is low-lying, covered with woods, and broken up into several regions by rivers and lagoons; but there is a shortage of water in some parts and the King pays people to furnish travellers with water; nobody would dare to take a drop without paying, and, if the official is not there, one leaves the money on the spot and continues on one's way. — O. DAPPER, a seventeenth-century Dutch merchant[31]

BENIN TODAY CONJURES up in the Western mind visions of brass sculpture, so treasured by European museums. Earlier in this century, Benin meant to the European a small West African kingdom where a massacre had taken place, one that was distorted and sensationalized in the press. But the Benin nation was far more than any of these parochial images suggest. It was, from the fifteenth through the seventeenth centuries, a city-state that achieved greatness and became a major political and cultural center in the midst of West Africa's forest region.

Many legends surround the beginnings of this unusual nation. One tells of Berber tribesmen, migrating from the northeast, settling in Benin and becoming its first rulers. Another indicates that the Edo peoples of Benin became disenchanted with their overlords and asked the legendary god, Oduduwa, to send his son, Oranmiyan, to govern their land. Oduduwa granted their request and, in the early fifteenth century, Oranmiyan was dispatched to Benin, where he organized the state. He took as his bride a Bini (Benin) princess who bore him a son. When the child came of age, Oranmiyan abdicated his throne and the boy became *oba* or king. So began the Benin dynasty.

A late sixteenth-century Dutch visitor compared Benin to his native Amsterdam:

> The towne [of Benin] seemeth to be very great, when you enter into it, you goe into a great broad street, not paved, which seemeth to be seven or eight times broader than the Warmoes street in Amsterdam; The King's Court is very great, within it having many great four-square Plaines, which round about them have Galleries, wherein there is alwaies watch kept.[32]

Benin's capital was encircled by an earth wall and ditch more than six miles in circumference. The town itself was divided into two parts, separated by the avenue described by the Dutch observer. The physical division was politically significant. The smaller of the districts contained the *oba's* residence and those of his closest advisers. The larger sub-division was inhabited by the minor officials, functionaries, and priests as well as the *Uzama*, the hereditary nobles who selected future rulers.

A century later, another Dutchman, Dapper, regarded the Benin people as "much more civilized than others on this [West African] coast. They are people who have good laws and a well-organized police; who live on good terms with the Dutch and other foreigners who come to trade among them, and show them a thousand marks of friendship."[33]

Benin remained a small kingdom for four centuries, until Oba Ewuare ascended the throne in 1440. Under Ewuare's leadership, Benin began to expand, absorbing neighboring communities, improving the trade routes so vital for its survival, and developing a political system which would later influence other West African forest states. The *oba*, assisted by the *Uzama*, was treated as if he were a divinity. Richard Eden, a sixteenth-century English traveler, commented on the esteem in which the *oba* was held by the people of Benin:

> The great reverence they give to their king, it is such, that if we would give as much to our Saviour Christ, we should remove from our heads many plagues which we daily deserve for our contempt and impietie. So it is therefore, that when his noble men are in his presence, they never look him in the face, but sit cowring . . . with their elbows upon their knees, and their hands before their faces, not looking up until the king command them. . . . Likewise, when they depart from him, they

turn not their backs toward him, but goe creeping back-
ward with like reverence.[34]

The *obas* who reigned after Ewuare looked beyond
the rain forest toward the coast to the Europeans
who had sailed to West Africa in search of ivory,
gold, and slaves. Oba Esigie (1504–1550) established trade relations with the Portuguese who, it is
believed, appeared in the Bight of Benin in the fifteenth century. The Portuguese chronicler, Ruy da
Pina, recorded these early contacts, noting:

> The King of Beny [Oba Esigie] sent as ambassador to
> the king a negro . . . because he desired to learn more
> about these lands, the arrival of people from them in his
> country being regarded as an unusual novelty. This am-
> bassador was a man of good speech and natural wisdom.[35]

The Benin merchants were admired for their business acumen throughout West Africa. Richard Eden
said of them that

> . . . they are very wary people in their bargaining, and
> will not lose one sparke of golde of any value. They use
> weights and measures [and] they that shall have to doe
> with them, must use them gently; for they will not tra-
> fique or bring in any wares, if they be evill used.[36]

Benin's civilization reached its highest point during the fifteenth and sixteenth centuries. Its progress and ultimate decline can almost be measured by
the changing style in her magnificent works of art.
The cherished Benin bronzes—heads, spears, and
swords—were first cast in the Yoruba spiritual center of Ife. The technique was passed on to Benin as

early, according to one source, as the thirteenth century. In the casting of brass, copper is a necessary ingredient, and it could be obtained only from the North. It was for this copper that Benin exchanged cotton, pepper, palm kernels, and slaves. Oba Esigie and his successors encouraged Benin's artistic labors. In 1540, he had a brass crucifix wrought and presented to the Portuguese king as a token of friendship. For three centuries, Benin's trade flourished with the Europeans and with other African nations.

Benin's prosperity eventually came to be based on the slave trade. While the enslavement of its own males was prohibited under earlier *obas*, intense competition with her rivals forced her kings to relax this prohibition in the seventeenth century. The slave traffic rooted itself more firmly and became Benin's paramount concern. It was this grim pursuit that hastened Benin's decline. The availability of firearms, imported by the Portuguese and first used in Oba Esigie's Benin, increased the conflict between her and her neighbors. In the seventeenth century, decay set in. This could be discerned in her art, which had by then lost its sensitivity and become more naturalistic and crude. Benin's control, which had once extended to the coast near Lagos and eastward to the Niger, was in jeopardy.

By the eighteenth century, the slave trade, as well as the frequent wars with her proliferating enemies combined to further undermine Benin's fast-disappearing strength. Benin was soon reduced

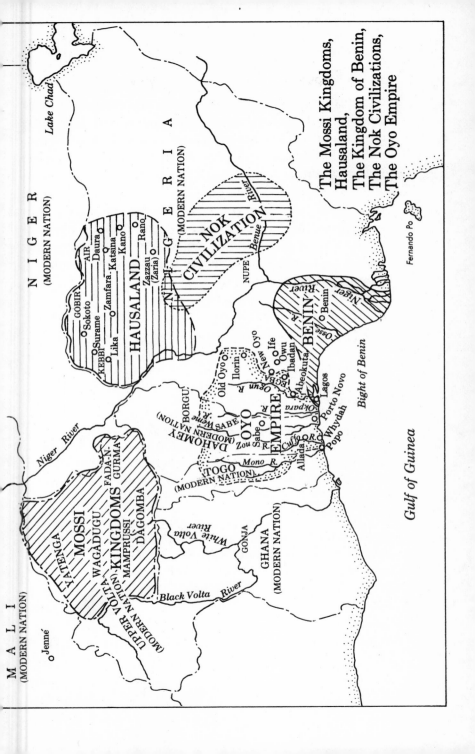

The Mossi Kingdoms, Hausaland,
The Kingdom of Benin,
The Nok Civilizations,
The Oyo Empire

to a minor state, attracting little attention until the British, during their imperial drive in the late nineteenth century, sought to place her under their "protection." The ruling *oba*, Overammi, balked, and the British sent an advance party to the city in 1897. The party was ambushed and its members were slain. Later in the year, Benin was captured, her priceless art treasures were stolen, and the *oba* was deposed and exiled. The overthrow of her monarchy and her occupation by the British marked the end of Benin as an independent nation.

THE ASHANTI

The king [*asantehene* Osei Bonsu], his tributaries, and captains were resplendent in the distance, surrounded by attendants of every description, fronted by a mass of warriors which seemed to make our approach impervious. . . . [the asantehene's] manners were majestic, yet courteous; and he did not allow his surprise to beguile him for a moment of the composure of the monarch. . . . He was seated in a low chair, richly ornamented in gold. . . . The royal stool [the Golden Stool] entirely cased in gold, was displayed under a splendid umbrella, with drums, sankos, horns, and various musical instruments, cased in gold, about the thickness of cartridge paper.—THOMAS BOWDICH, the British envoy to Kumasi, 1817[37]

MANY NATIONS THAT achieved greatness in West Africa did so by their access to the trade

routes which crossed the Western Sudan and connected inland Africa with the forest and the sea.
Trade is every nation's lifeline and the Ashanti were
no exception. Some historians have proposed that
the Ashanti first settled around Tafo, the fork from
which caravan routes branched toward Hausaland
and the Western Sudan. The Ashanti are descended
from the Akan peoples, who are thought to have
emigrated to the Ghana-Nigeria area in the thirteenth century. The Akan evolved, according to one
historian, in the region between the Black Volta
(Ghana) and the Comoe (Ivory Coast) rivers. Others
attribute their origin to North Africa, Mesopotamia,
and even ancient Ghana, one thousand miles to the
north. Whatever their ancestry, the Akan were
nation-makers of a type that West Africa had rarely
seen. The most important of the numerous states
that sprang from Akan origins were the Ashanti.

Until the seventeenth century, Ashanti was a
cluster of small, feeble states. This makeup changed
under their first recorded ruler, Obiri Yeboa, in the
middle of the century. He brought together the
Ashanti settlements in the Kumasi district and, in
effect, the Ashanti nation was born. However, Ashanti was still dominated by its larger southern neighbor, Denkyira, another Akan state.

The Dutch, by competing with the Portuguese for
control of the lucrative Guinea slave and gold trade,
probably provided the spark — in the form of firearms — that set in motion Ashanti's revolt against
Denkyira. Ashanti was, from its inception to its fall
in the nineteenth century, the center of a continuous

arms race. For the better part of two centuries, Ashanti would find herself matched against her neighbors, either in battle for survival, or as the pawn of one or another European imperial power.

The most memorable of Ashanti's early rulers was Osei Tutu, the king of Kumasi. As a youth, he was apprenticed to the Denkyira court. He later departed and for a time lived in Akwamu, a rival of Denkyira. In the 1960s, Osei Tutu returned to his native Kumasi, accompanied by a band of advisers, the chief of whom was the priest and magician, Okomfo Anokye.

Osei Tutu was bent on uniting the Ashanti and freeing his people from Denkyira's rule. To achieve his aim, it was first necessary to attain undisputed leadership among the other Ashanti kings. This was a task in which Okomfo Anokye would prove to be of invaluable assistance. For the Ashanti, the symbol of royalty and divinity, the object in which the mystique of the Ashanti nation resides, is the Golden Stool. Legend has it that at a meeting of Ashanti's leaders a thunderclap was heard and the now revered Golden Stool descended from the heavens and landed next to Osei Tutu. Okomfo Anokye immediately proclaimed that the stool was the repository of Ashanti's soul and symbolized a unified Ashanti nation. So startled and impressed by the event were the other Ashanti rulers that Osei Tutu was popularly acclaimed *asantehene*, or king, of the Ashanti. Kumasi was chosen as the capital of the Ashanti nation. Osei Tutu was committed to rule with the advice and consent of the heads of Ashanti's sister states, the *omanhene*, each of whom were compelled to swear allegiance to the *asantehene*. Thus the Ashanti nation was born.

The problem of Denkyira's hegemony over Ashanti, however, remained. When, in 1698, she again demanded tribute, Osei Tutu turned to Akwamu for military aid. The combined armies of the two Akan nations overwhelmed the forces of Denkyira. By 1701, Ashanti freedom had been won and, along with it, access to the sea. This military windfall included the land rights to Elmina, the Dutch trading "castle" on the Gold Coast (Ghana). Following the successful struggle against Denkyira, Osei Tutu created political alliances in order to strengthen his insurgent empire. But his death by ambush in 1712 aborted Osei Tutu's empire-building.

Fortunately, the Ashanti empire remained in able hands as Osei Tutu's nephew, Opaku Ware, eventually succeeded his uncle as *asantehene*. His rule, which began in 1720 and lasted until 1750, was notable for its conquests and territorial expansion. Under Opaku Ware, the threat from Denkyira was completely eliminated by the 1720s and the *asantehene* turned against the Mossi nations north of Ashanti. The prize of the gold, ivory, and kola nut trade beckoned and Opaku Ware rode against Dagomba, the Mossi guardian of the trade routes. His armies met with disorganized opposition and these nations were made Ashanti tributaries in Opaku Ware's growing nation. In the meantime, the enemy

Akim state had subdued Akwamu in 1730, capturing the port of Accra. For Opaku Ware, this was an unsettling situation, which endangered Ashanti hegemony, obstructed her access to the coast, and affected her massive trade in slaves which she sold to the waiting European buyers. In 1744, Opaku Ware's armies struck, crushing Akim and reaching the sea once more. Ashanti had become, by the second half of the eighteenth century, an empire of 150,000 square miles, stretching in the north to Dagomba and Mamprussi and along the coast from Cape Mount (Liberia) to Dahomey. An estimate of its population places it at anywhere from three to five millions. The *asantehene* had arrogated to himself many of the political and financial rights formerly reserved for the *omanhene*. Osei Kwame, the *asantehene* who reigned from 1777 to 1801, had Europeans among his advisers, and the Hausa states as well as the Fulani and Dahomeans sent envoys to his court. With control over the coast and the northern gold-producing areas, Ashanti had become West Africa's foremost power.

Despite her new-found status, Ashanti's enemies did not disappear. Her most serious rival were the Fanti, whose authority extended over most of the Gold Coast east of the Ashanti-held regions, including the English trading depots of Cape Coast Castle and Anomabu.

In 1700, the Fanti peoples had banded together in a loose defense-oriented confederation. This organization was presumably created as a counterforce to the Ashanti. Its primary aim was to prevent the Ashanti from gaining control over the entire Gold Coast.

The Europeans were willing to support, within limits, the West African nation that would grant them the most agreeable trading terms. An added element, which further complicated Ashanti-Fanti relations, was the intense commercial battle between the British and the Dutch. The Dutch naturally favored the Ashanti, from whom they leased the coastal depot of Elmina. The British, on the other hand, were partial to the Fanti, whom they viewed as a wedge between their coastal forts and the hostile Ashanti nation. In any event, the stage was prepared for the first of many Ashanti-Fanti wars.

The Ashanti would probably have marched against the Fanti before the nineteenth century but they were delayed, preoccupied instead with incorporating their conquered lands into their empire. Also, at the end of the eighteenth century, the Ashanti were faced with uprisings in Muslim communities within their domain as the *jihad* of the Muslim reformer and revolutionary, Uthman dan Fodio, gathered steam.

In 1806, the Fanti-Ashanti issue came to a head. Ashanti refugees had sought asylum with the Fanti. The ruling *asantehene*, Osei Bonsu (1801–24), demanded that they be returned to Kumasi but his request was ignored. This was a slight that the *asantehene* could not let pass and, too, it provided a pretext for invasion. Much to the chagrin of their English allies, the Fanti were quickly overrun. Only an outbreak of smallpox among the Ashanti saved the Fanti from annihilation. For the next fifteen years, the British watched helplessly as the Ashanti-Fanti conflict continued. While her trade was imperiled and the cost of her coastal administration was rising, Britain was reluctant to involve itself deeply in Ashanti-Fanti affairs. In London, the voices for withdrawal from West Africa rang loud and clear. The crowning embarrassment came in 1824 when the governor of Sierra Leone, Sir Charles MacCarthy, incensed at Ashanti's slave-trading operations, took matters into his own hands. With a small force, he challenged Osei Bonsu's imposing army. The outcome of this impulsive action was never in question. MacCarthy and his band proved no contest for the superior Ashanti forces and MacCarthy himself was killed. The floodgates holding back the tide of opposition to Great Britain's West African ventures were now opened. Opinion in Parliament favored a general pullback but, in 1828, a compromise with the increasing number of West African palm oil traders, who opposed any reduction in British representation on the coast, was reached. Thereafter, the British combined their West African territories, leaving the merchants to administer the coastal depots, aided by a government subsidy.

In 1830, the Committee of London Merchants, as this circle of Gold Coast traders was known, appointed George Maclean, a former army officer, to work out a truce with the Ashanti. Maclean did far more than negotiate an agreement. His well-deserved reputation for fairness enabled him to develop a rapport with the Ashanti and, within a short time, Maclean became the *de facto* legal authority in the region, arbitrating disputes between English traders and among the Ashanti themselves. During his reign on the Gold Coast, he persuaded the Ashanti to relinquish their traditional rights to the coastal forts, concluded a peace between the Ashanti and their arch enemies, the Fanti, and brought to the Gold Coast a period of unprecedented tranquillity. Consequently, British trade improved steadily.

But the British government feared that Maclean and the merchants were involving themselves too deeply in native affairs. In 1843, they relieved the merchants of their administrative responsibilities and resumed direct jurisdiction over the Gold Coast's forts. A year later, they concluded a "bond" with the Fanti which came to be regarded as a committment by Great Britain to act as the tribe's protector. In effect, the British government was doing exactly what they had counseled the merchants and Maclean against doing—they were involving themselves in the tribal affairs of the Gold Coast's peoples.

British relations with the Ashanti began to deteriorate once more. The British attitude toward slaving, upon which the Ashanti economy depended, and her blockade of suspected West African slave trade ports, made even more precarious the relations between the two nations.

In 1863, once more using the pretext of seeking Ashanti fugitives who had reached safety on the coast, the Ashanti made another foray against the Fanti. The reaction in Parliament to this new incursion was the same as it had been in the 1820s. Many members were convinced that withdrawal was the only course to follow. A Special Committee of Parliament, organized to investigate the West African situation, recommended that the British abandon all of West Africa with the exception of Sierra Leone. What the British did instead was once again to combine their West African possessions. The Fanti, however, viewed the British move with alarm. They had been betrayed in their time of need once before by their so-called ally. To avoid a repetition of the disaster of 1806 at the hands of the Ashanti, the Fanti met, in 1871, at their capital of Mankessim to form another alliance in case the British actually did leave West Africa. Great Britain, however, accused the Fanti of an anti-British conspiracy. The Fanti leaders were arrested and the new federation was thus destroyed. Fortunately for the Fanti, abandonment was not in the cards. The British ploughed ahead, trading off some of their coastal enclaves for others, cementing as best they could their control of coastal trade. The French had, by this time, made their debut in areas bordering on the British colony of Sierra Leone and all signs pointed to further French movement inland. All these factors entered into the British decision to reject the suggestions of the Special Committee and pursue a forward policy in West Africa.

The Ashanti were drawn into battle again in 1873. The issue this time was a false document, with the forged signature of the ruling Ashanti *asantehene*, Kofi Karikari, which purported to relinquish his traditional rights to Elmina. Both the British and the Dutch, who occupied the fort, accepted the document as genuine. Kofi Karikari, enraged at this forgery and the British unquestioning acceptance of it, mounted a campaign against them in 1873. A repeat of the smallpox epidemic of 1806 and heavy rains halted the Ashanti advance. The delay gave the British and the Fanti time to catch their breath. When hostilities were resumed, the better-prepared British army under Major-General Sir Garnet Wolseley crushed the depleted Ashanti forces and took Kumasi. The region south of Ashanti, including the coastal ports, was annexed and, in 1874, the Gold Coast colony was declared. Kofi Karikari was deposed and a new *asantehene*, Mensah Bonsu, was installed in 1875.

Mensah Bonsu lasted until 1883 when he was destooled by the younger, more radical Ashanti, who considered the *asantehene* a British puppet. From 1883 until the accession of Prempeh I to the Ashanti throne in 1888, the nation was embroiled in civil war. From the very beginning of his reign, the new *asantehene* was governed by a desire to regain for Ashanti its lost lands and past glories. On Ashanti's borders, French and German treaty-making began to unnerve the British. In response, to prevent their colonial rivals from gaining a foothold in Ashanti itself, they suggested a protectorate to Prempeh in

1890. Prempeh, after due consideration, rejected the offer.

In 1893, Prempeh's success in regaining many of the districts lost to Ashanti through defection persuaded the British that they had best clip his wings. They demanded that he end his campaign to restore the breakaway regions to Ashanti and, in addition, permit a British resident in Kumasi. Prempeh stalled, sailing instead to Great Britain with an entourage to plead his case for independence before Parliament.

The colorful scheme failed, for the Gold Coast's British governor, Frederick Hodgson, had by this time decided that Prempeh must be removed from the Ashanti throne. The failure of Prempeh to reply satisfactorily to an ultimatum that he accept the British resident was used as an excuse for the January 1896 invasion of Ashanti. There was little bloodshed, for Prempeh and his people chose not to resist. The *asantehene* was arrested, along with the queen mother and other members of the royal court, and deported to Sierra Leone and then, in 1900, to the Seychelles.

The crowning indignity to the Ashanti people came in 1900 when Hodgson demanded the surrender of the Golden Stool and announced his intention to sit upon it. Even when an *asantehene* is enstooled, he is raised and lowered above the stool but he is never permitted to sit upon it. This greatest affront to all that was sacred to the Ashanti was the last straw. Hodgson had assumed that without the Golden

Stool, the Ashanti could not enstool an *asantehene* around whom they could rally. They would, therefore, according to Hodgson's logic, be divided and more easily controlled. But the governor misjudged the Ashanti. They revolted and Hodgson had to struggle back to the safety of Accra.

Ashanti was not the only scene of bloody disturbances during the last years of the nineteenth and the first decade of the twentieth century. Oppressive British policies caused outbreaks in Sierra Leone, the Niger Delta, and Benin as well. In Ashanti, as elsewhere, each uprising was suppressed. In 1901, Ashanti became part of Great Britain's Gold Coast colony. Her valiant struggle to retain her independence was at an end.

THE KINGDOM OF DAHOMEY

The Dahomans were formerly called Foys, and inhabited a small territory, on the northeast part of their present kingdom, whose capital, Dawhee, lay between the towns of Calmina and Abomey, at about 90 miles from the seacoast. — ARCHIBALD DALZELL, *History of Dahomey*, 1793[38]

IN THE EARLY seventeenth century, following a dynastic dispute among the Aja members of the

Allada royal house (located in modern Togo), the two youngest pretenders to the Tado throne fled the kingdom. The eldest prince remained and successfully exerted his claim to the monarchy. His dissident brothers founded the rival kingdoms of Abomey or Dahomey and Porto Novo, an enclave on the Atlantic coast.

Some scholars have written that by the mid-seventeenth century, the alien Aja tribesmen had intermarried with the local Yoruba peoples and their offspring came to be known as the Foys or Fon. Although Fon origins have never been precisely determined, a strong cultural connection links the Fon and Yoruba, many of whom settled in Dahomey when it was under Oyo's hegemony.

From its early years, Dahomey was a restless nation, conquering its neighbors and extending its boundaries in all directions. Dahomey's third king was believed to have been Wegbaja (1650–85), the grandson of the founder of Dahomey. While it was Wegbaja who established the ruling dynasty, it was under Akaba (1685–1708) and Agaja (1708–40), that Dahomey was set on its aggressive course.

Dahomey's military reputation was awesome and, in later times, somewhat undeserved. Yet it was this overblown image of strength that instilled fear among her more powerful rivals.

In the eighteenth century, Dahomey had in fact organized a formidable army with the intention of overthrowing the Aja states which enclosed it like a vise. From 1724 to 1734, Dahomey frequently

clashed with Allada. During this decade, too,
Whydah and Jakin on the coast fell to Agaja's cavalry.
The flourishing slave trade was temporarily prohibited by the Dahomean king, who feared it would
weaken his growing nation by depopulating it of
much needed manpower.

As we have seen, Dahomey's advances and policies did not escape the notice of Oyo. The great
Yoruba power viewed Dahomey as a dangerous up-
start nation, directly threatening its own substantial
empire, of which Dahomey was considered a part.
Oyo moved against Dahomey, a campaign undertaken between 1726 and 1740. During this period,
Oyo raided Dahomey on four occasions. Robert
Norris, whose reminiscences of Dahomey were published fifty years later, described one Oyo invasion:

> To the northeast of Dahomey lies a fine, fertile and
> extensive country, inhabited by a great and warlike peo-
> ple, called the [Oyos]; the scourge and terror of all their
> neighbours. . . . They invaded Dahomey in 1738 with an
> irresistible army, and laid the country waste with fire and
> sword to the gates of Abomey; here the Foys [Fons] had
> collected their whole strength, and waited the arrival of
> the enemy, who were advancing with an incredible multi-
> tude.[39]

While the Dahomeans were not easily intimidat-
ed, they were not yet a match for the Oyos and soon
found themselves retreating into Abomey, their capital, portrayed by Norris as "a very large town, surrounded with a deep moat, but has no wall nor
breastwork to defend the besieged; nor are there

any springs of water in it; consequently it could not be tenable." The Dahomeans evacuated the town, taking with them the king's treasures, and left it to be plundered and burned by the invaders. The Oyo harassment of the Dahomeans continued until an accommodation was reached with Oyo in 1830 and Dahomey was reduced to tributary status.

Despite her defeat, many of Dahomey's coastal possessions were retained and the Europeans who traded there had to secure special permits from the Dahomean king. Under Agaja, the European slave houses were burned to the ground in an effort to stem the trade. While the Dahomean monarch may have considered slave trading a danger to his nation's stability, he soon underwent a change of heart and lifted the increasingly unpopular prohibition. During the reigns of his successors, Tegbesu IV (1740–74) and Kpengla (1774–89), slaves in unprecedented numbers were taken and exchanged for European firearms. During the last quarter of the eighteenth century, slavery became the lifeblood of Dahomey's economy, increasing in importance in proportion to the European demand for plantation labor.

Simultaneously, Dahomey's struggle with her overlord, Oyo, intensified, too. While Oyo had been progressively weakened through wars and internal disputes, she still demanded a greater share of tribute and competed with Dahomey for control over the coastal areas. When Dahomey stepped up her raids on the ports of Badagry and Porto Novo, Oyo found it difficult to intercede on their behalf.

In 1797, a severe economic depression struck Dahomey. The effect was so unsettling and devastating that the nation's disgruntled subjects rose in revolt and assassinated the king, Agonglo. A futile effort to change the dynasty ended when Agonglo's son, Adandozan (1797–1818), grabbed the reins of power and restored order. While political stability was to some extent restored, the economic chaos lingered. After 1808, Great Britain's abolition of the slave trade aggravated Dahomey's deteriorating economy. British cruisers patrolled the coast in search of violators; many a slaver was intercepted and its cargo freed in Sierra Leone. Though it became more difficult to slip slaves past the British blockade, the slave market in Brazil picked up some of the slack. But, clearly, her dependence on the slave trade had placed Dahomey in a commercial straitjacket.

It was only when Gezo (1818–1858) overthrew Adandozan that Dahomey recovered some of her imperial stature. In 1821, this formidable warrior-king won Dahomey's independence from Oyo, which was crippled and in decline. Gezo's court flourished, particularly with the assistance and advice of a Brazilian mulatto from Whydah named Souza. Many descendants of slaves originally transported to Brazil by Dahomey returned to the African coast and established themselves as merchants. Souza was reported to be one of these repatriates. During Gezo's time, Dahomey drifted away from the increasingly unpopular slave trade and into the cultivation of oil palms and the exporting of palm oil, which in the nineteenth century replaced slaves as West Africa's major commodity.

While Dahomey shone in the glow of new-found imperial power, her eastern neighbors, the Egba, threatened her empire by occupying an area into which Dahomey had hoped to expand. These Yoruba peoples, who had defected from Oyo's crumbling empire, made Abeokuta their capital. Still another problem was posed by the Egbado whose kingdom straddled the route to the former slave port of Badagry. Gezo moved intermittently against his rivals in 1842, but with little success. The Egba, many of whom had been educated by missionaries in the coastal settlements, were supplied with weapons by the British. Great Britain's intention was to neutralize Dahomey which could disrupt the growing trade in palm oil by cutting it off at its source.

In 1851, a Dahomean army of 16,000 men and women marched on Abeokuta. Dahomey had underestimated its enemy and the Dahomean force was shattered by the well-prepared Egba. One English observer commented that "this affair spoiled the terrible name of the Dahomies." Dahomey's reputation as a fighting nation did not survive the battle, though she would again try her luck against the Egba.

Upon Gezo's death in 1858, his son, Gelele, vowed to continue the campaign against the Egba. In 1864, Gelele, like his father before him, was robbed of vengeance by the superior Egba army. Richard Burton, the English traveler and scholar, was in

Dahomey as Gelele's followers left for battle. As the female contingent known to the Dahomeans as "our mothers" passed, Burton recorded his impressions:

> The officers, distinguished by their white head-cloths, and by an esquires-at-arms, generally a small slave girl, [carried] a musket, [leading] their commands. . . . The privates carried packs on cradles, like those of the male soldiery, containing their bed-mats, clothes, and food for a week or a fortnight, mostly toasted grains and bean-cake, hot with peppers. Cartridge-pouches of two different shapes were girt round their waists, and slung to their sides were water-gourds, fetish-sacks, bullet-wallets, powder-calabashes, fans, little cutlasses, wooden pipe-cases enveloped in leather tobacco-bags, flint, steel, and tinder, and Lilliputian stools, with three or four legs, cut out of single blocks.[40]

Despite their numbers, Dahomey suffered another crushing defeat. The prize of Abeokuta was to elude Dahomey forever.

Dahomey's troubles with her neighbors were minor compared with what was yet to come. In 1892, her ninth and last independent king, Gelele's son Behanzin, known to his people as Kondo ("the Shark"), was confronted with the French. France was then locked in an imperial race with Great Britain and Dahomey lay in her path. The French declared war on Dahomey and within a year Abomey fell. Behanzin fled, his capital in flames. In 1894, with his back to the wall, Behanzin was deposed by French General Alfred Dodds, a mulatto of Senegalese descent, and the kingdom of Dahomey was added to France's growing colonial empire.

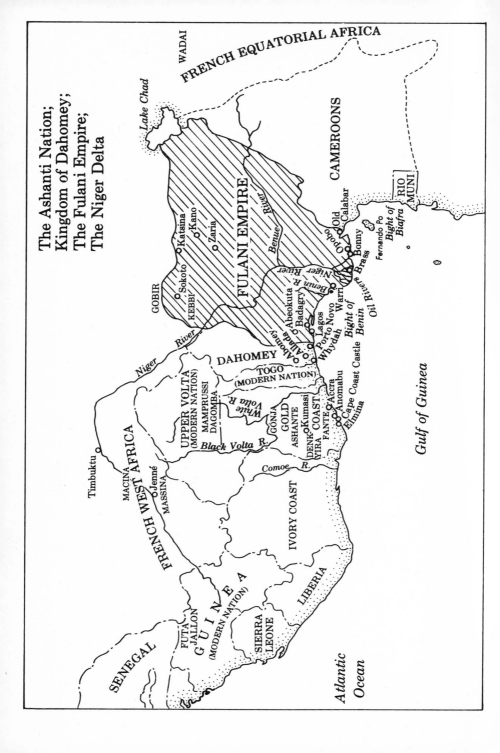

The Ashanti Nation;
Kingdom of Dahomey;
The Fulani Empire;
The Niger Delta

THE FULANI

Know that he [Uthman dan Fodio] grew up continent and devout, possessed of pleasing qualities. And none was his equal. People trusted him,
and flocked to him from east and west.
— MUHAMMAD BELLO describing his father,
Uthman dan Fodio.[41]

FEW PEOPLES HAVE had as diverse and checkered a history as the Fulani of West Africa. Their
origins have remained a mystery. However, their
traditions do differ from their West African brothers,
which indicates that they are not indigenous to
the areas that they occupy today. It has been suggested that the Fulani dwelled in ancient Ghana
as early as the seventh century. In the eleventh
century, however, the Almoravide invasions drove
these pastoralists from Ghana to the south and
east. Despite their role as cattle breeders and
suppliers to the markets of West Africa, the Fulani,
too, had designs for conquest. Their quest for
new territory brought them into conflict with the
great armies of Mansa Musa and Sunni Ali, and
against them the nomadic Fulani fared badly. Elsewhere, in Macina, Kebbi, and Kaniaga, their numbers and influence prevailed and they dominated
these nation states. Much of their success was short-
lived, however, as they often became the pawn of
other, more durable West African empires.

As they began to settle in the towns of West
Africa, the Fulani engaged in trade and crafts as well

as cattle raising. By the thirteenth century, a large concentration of Fulani could be found in Futa Jallon (in Guinea) while many others had wandered as far east as modern Cameroon.

It was between the fifteen and eighteenth centuries that the Fulani changed from being occasional warriors and became a perpetual threat to their neighbors' survival. Mounted calvary and the introduction of European firearms combined to turn the Fulani into a military force. In 1559, they overthrew their Soninke overlords in Futa Toro. There, and in Futa Jallon and Macina, the Fulani began to develop into more than a widespread, disconnected tribe of horsemen and pastoralists. It was also in these centers that Islam eventually took root and altered the course of West African history.

In the eighteenth century the tranquillity of Europe was disturbed by the ominous rumblings of revolution. In West Africa, too, a political and economic revolution was brewing, no less violent and important for Africa than the French Revolution was for Europe. A *jihad*, or holy war, under the unifying banner of Islam, was in the wind. Its leader was the scholar-soldier, Uthman dan Fodio.

Born in 1754 in a Fulani village in Hausaland's Gobir, Uthman served as a tutor to the sons of Gobir's rulers. One of these princes, Yunfa, would become Uthman's hated adversary. While his popularity among the Muslim faithful was unquestioned, Uthman's demands for reform and an end to corruption presented a problem for Gobir's rulers. Uthman had no hesitation about going beyond the limits of his position when he thought he was acting in the Muslims' interest. An attempt was made to assassinate him in 1789, and when Uthman attempted to intercede on behalf of imprisoned Muslims, he brought the wrath of the court down upon his head and had to flee Gobir. His journey was later compared, by his evergrowing and faithful following, with Muhammad's *hegira* to Mecca in 532 A.D.

Uthman could sense the considerable support for his movement, especially among the long-suffering Muslim poor. He had toyed with the idea of a *jihad* for at least a decade. Now, from the unemployed of the Futa Toro, Macina, and Songhai communities, he raised an army and, after his election as *Sarkin Musulmi*, or Commander of the Faithful, marched forth to bring the word of Allah to Islam's pagan enemies. As the *shehu*, or sultan, of all Fulani, he sent flags — the symbol of holy war — to his compatriots. The flag empowered those who received it to act for the sultan in proclaiming and pursuing a *jihad*.

Yunfa, who had forced Uthman to leave Gobir, was the first to taste defeat in 1804. The rulers of Zaria suffered next. But, with the assistance of the Tauregs, Gobir's army regrouped and turned back a Fulani assault in 1805. This Hausa victory was merely an unpleasant interlude for the zealous Uthman. In 1806, the Fulani recovered, crushed the Taureg, and the shaky Hausa defenses crumbled. Two years later, Yunfa died in battle and Uthman's revenge, so to speak, was complete.

By 1808, the Fulani standard flew over Kano, Katsina, Zana, and Sokoto. In each case, an *emir*, or ruler, was appointed to govern the Hausa nation-state, a
political device which would be used in other
Fulani-conquered lands. In 1809, Uthman dan Fodio, whose lightning military thrusts changed the
political face of West Africa, decided to retire from
active politics. The remaining eight years of his life
would be devoted to his beloved Islamic religion.

While Uthman exploited to the fullest the cause
of Islam, he took equal pains to play up the economic oppression and dislocation of the Muslim
masses and thus inflame them against their non-
Muslim overlords. When the military aspects of the
revolution succeeded, Uthman intended to recon-
struct Fulani government according to specific
idealistic principles. Rule was henceforth to be based
upon consultation, and power was to be kept from
those who too actively sought it. Justice, good works,
and understanding were to govern the ruler's relations with his people. The ideals of Uthman's constitution were admirable. Unfortunately, despotism
in the Fulani-controlled lands became once more
the rule rather than the exception. The lot of the
Muslim masses after Uthman's revolution improved
little.

In 1812, three years after he had removed himself
from the Fulani political scene, Uthman's empire
was divided into two parts. The eastern section fell
to Muhammad Bello, Uthman's son, who ruled from
Sokoto. Bello, who had occupied Sokoto since
1807, assumed the title of *musulmi*. The western sec-

tor went to Uthman's brother, Abdullahi, then *emir* of Gwandu.

Muhammad Bello was described by a contemporary writer as having a "ruddy complexion, tall, bald of head, [and] wearing a . . . tufted beard" and was credited with spreading a "respect for learning." According to the observer, under Bello, "the Hausa country flourished greatly," and "scholars came from different countries."[42] Muhammad Bello's reputation as a scholar outshines his abilities as a warrior. Plagued by the Kanemi of Bornu and others, Bello barely managed to maintain his empire. He is remembered more for his qualities as a man of letters than as a soldier. In 1837, Muhammad Bello died and his brother, Atiku (1837–1842) became sultan of Sokoto. Atiku was regarded as a humorless puritan, and his rule was spotted with uprisings in Gobir and Katsina. This was the legacy left to his nephew, Muhammad Bello's son, Aliu Baba, who reigned from 1842 to 1859.

Elsewhere in the polyglot, loosely connected Fulani empire, other leaders, encouraged by Uthman's success, hoisted the standard of revolt. Among them was Séku Ahmadu Lobo from Macina, who proclaimed a *jihad* in 1810. By 1844, Séku Ahmadu's empire stretched from Jenné to Timbuktu in the Western Sudan. He died in 1844 and was succeeded by his son, Ahmadu II, under whom the kingdom collapsed before the armies of El-Hajj Umar, an Islamic preacher and soldier from Futa Toro.

El-Hajj Umar made the obligatory pilgrimage to

Mecca in 1825 and, upon his return, married the daughter of Muhammad Bello of Sokoto. In 1839, he established his headquarters at Futa Jallon. At the time of his death in 1864 at Macina, El-Hajj Umar's kingdom reached from Senegal to Timbuktu.

El-Hajj Umar's son and successor, Ahmadu Séku, was as acquisitive as his father. But a new element was introduced which affected Ahmadu Séku's plans for adding new lands to his imperial legacy. The French had penetrated into the Senegal valley and Ahmadu Séku's dream of empire was rudely shattered.

The imperial road had its obstructions for the French, however. Their greatest nemesis was an empire builder named Samori Touré, the son of a humble trader, born in the early 1830s. Samori harbored the vision of an enormous empire and by 1873 neared his lifelong goal. A year later, he adopted the title of *almami*, the equivalent of Uthman's *shehu*, and began to move from his capital at Bissandugu (in Guinea) toward the north. Hampered by the French who sought to control as much of West Africa as possible before their British rivals did so, Samori realized his only chance for survival lay in playing off one European power against another. In true diplomatic fashion, he offered to place himself under British protection, in 1885, in exchange for sorely needed firearms. Unfortunately, Samori's plan backfired as the cautious British hesitated. The French, fearful of a British occupation of the Niger region, presented to them a forged docu-

ment purporting to be Samori's acceptance of
French protection. The British unaccountably believed the French ruse. Samori and his followers
rejected the forgery for what it was and once more
took up arms against the French. His guerrilla tac-
tics had little effect, though, and Samori eventually
realized he was fighting a losing battle. In 1898, he
was persuaded to negotiate a truce with the French
during which he was betrayed, captured, and exiled.
In 1900, Samori Touré died.

The Fulani leaders who ruled after Aliu Baba
from 1859 were unable to cope with the European
advance into their territories. The empires and tributaries of the various sultans were chipped away by
the British and French. Within their own domains,
they suffered from civil strife, aided by the constant
warfare which became a part of nineteenth-century
West African life.

The British pressed the campaign against the
remaining independent Fulani emirates. One by one
they began to defect from Sokoto, the fulcrum upon
which the Fulani empire was balanced, and to which
Fulani leaders owed their allegiance. In 1902, the
British moved against the last holdout, Attahiru, the
sultan of Sokoto.

Attahiru had persistently refused to buckle under
the onrush of colonialism. But the British were not
to be denied. They despatched an expedition to
Sokoto in 1903, where they overwhelmed Attahiru's
army. The sultan had to flee, but the situation within
his sultanate had so changed that it was difficult for

him to gain refuge. Finally, he decided to make a stand in Burmi, southeast of Sokoto. As the British breached Burmi's walls, Attahiru came forth to face them and was killed. With the death of Attahiru, the colonial partition of West Africa into colonies and protectorates, to all intents and purposes, neared completion.

THE NIGER DELTA

West Africa is essentially a land of oils; this is its real wealth; and the exports of ivory and gold are small in comparison. . . . Among the whites there is no real unity: nobody trusts his neighbour. This gives the blacks a great advantage. . . . Rivals as they are, they can at least combine with that honesty which is always the best policy. — W. WINWOOD READE, a British traveler in West Africa, 1863.[43]

THE NIGER DELTA lies 250 miles east of Lagos on the Gulf of Guinea. Vast stretches of the region are overgrown with mangrove vegetation while swamps, lagoons, and an interconnecting web of creeks and streams pit the coastline. The area's innumerable natural hiding places provided shelter from British anti-slaving patrols for the swift canoes of the illegal slavers well into the nineteenth century. It was from the slave trade, which Great Britain abolished in 1808, that many of the Delta's peoples prospered. Eventually, as the American slave markets were closed off, the Delta's slave traders used their talents to build up the increasingly important trade in the palm products of Nigeria's forested interior.

By the seventeenth century, many tribes had settled in the Niger Delta. The Ijaw preceded the neighboring Efik, Urhobo, Ibeno, Kalabari, and Itsekiri tribes. These traditional fishermen soon found they could enrich themselves faster by selling slaves to the Europeans. As the slave trade died out, they became middlemen, intermediaries between the Europeans who anchored their ships in the Delta and the Ibo palm oil suppliers of the hinterland.

The Ibo, who made their home in Nigeria's eastern region, differed from many of West Africa's ethnic groups in a number of respects. Their communities were not monarchies. They were knit together spiritually and governed loosely by councils of elders. It can be said that a rough form of democracy existed in Iboland. A branch of the Ibo, the Aro, whom the parent tribe called the "Umu-Chukwu," or Children of God, were the traditional guardians of the Long Juju, the sacred Ibo shrine which was located at Arochukwu. When the British occupied Iboland in 1902, they destroyed the shrine.

The Aro used their unique spiritual position to dominate first the slave and later the palm markets of eastern Nigeria. Scores of captives would be offered up by Aro priests as a sacrifice to the Long Juju. Or they might be exacted as fines in payment

for misdeeds. Either way, the result was the same.
The unfortunate individual would soon find himself
sold as a slave to the coastal middleman who in turn
would re-sell him to a European bidder.

The most striking feature of the Niger Delta during the eighteenth and nineteenth centuries was the
"house system." A "house" was essentially a commercial arrangement organized by the Delta's tribes
to fulfill the demand for slaves and palm oil. Each
house had a chief, a sub-chief, a corps of freemen,
and slaves. A house member, whether he be slave or
free, could become head of a house. This upward
social mobility caused bitter internal power strug-
gles which weakened the stability of many houses.

These houses formed the basis for the Niger Delta's numerous city-states, Warri, Brass, Akassa,
Creek Town, Old and New Calabar, and Bonny
among them. Bonny, at the Delta's mouth, was its
most important city-state for much of the nineteenth
century. The Englishman Winwood Reade visited
Bonny and later described the manner in which
palm oil trading was conducted in his memoir, *Savage Africa* (1863):

> We entered Bonny, the wealthiest of these rivers. . . .
> Here the traders do not dare to live ashore but inhabit
> the huge huge hulks of ancient merchantmen. . . . The
> trade [in palm oil] is active enough, but from its nature
> is attended with much delay. The Bonny natives go to
> [the Ibo-controlled] market in the interior. The oil is
> brought to them little by little in calabashes. This they
> pour off into barrels. It is then brought on board one of
> the hulks, and is purchased with goods of European man-
> ufacture.[44]

During the formative years of the palm oil trade, Europeans and the Delta peoples shared an equality based upon mutual necessity. Captain John Adams, a nineteenth-century British mariner, detailed his impressions of life in Old Calabar, where the value of education was recognized by English merchant and African alike:

> Many of the natives write English; an art first acquired by some of the traders' sons, who had visited England, and which they have had the sagacity to retain up to the present period. They have established schools and schoolmasters, for the purpose of instructing in this art the youths belonging to families of consequence.[45]

When, in industrializing England, the demand for palm oil as a machine lubricant expanded, the courtesies of the past were discarded. As English traders poured into the Delta in the 1830s, competition intensified and so too did the incidence of bloodshed. The Europeans tried to eliminate the middlemen by going directly to the inland palm markets, but the Delta houses protested and, with their livelihood at stake, frequently attacked these commercial expeditions. The English merchants responded by petitioning Parliament for protection. Great Britain, still in its "reluctant imperialist" stage, had serious reservations about any West African involvement, but they could not long ignore these traders' complaints, especially when it affected the British pocketbook.

The British found they could not exempt themselves from Delta politics forever. The turning

point came in 1849 when John Beecroft, who had
once served as governor of the island of Fernando
Po, was appointed consul for the Bights of Benin
and Biafra. Beecroft was a man committed to the
extension of British influence along the Gulf of
Guinea's coastline, to the killing off forever of the
still active slave trade, and to ensuring the safety
and comfort of the English palm oil merchants. During the five years of his consularship, he redirected
and transformed Great Britain's Niger Delta policy.
Whereas the British government preferred to remain aloof from the affairs of the Delta city-states,
Beecroft took it upon himself to intervene wherever
and whenever the opportunity presented itself.

In Old Calabar, where abuses of slaves made an
insurrection inevitable, Beecroft stepped into the
dispute and, in his own words, "succeeded in concil-
iating the Insurgents, and amicably settling [the is-
sue]." Between 1849 and 1854, Beecroft had removed King Aqua of Old Calabar, presided over the
Court of Equity which exiled King William Pepple
of Bonny, and had King Kosuku of Lagos dethroned.
Each ruler was replaced with a man of Beecroft's
choosing. By the time the consul died, the pendu-
lum of power in the Niger Delta had swung irrevoc-
ably toward Great Britain.

The Delta city-states still had to be reckoned with
despite the deep inroads made during Beecroft's
time. The confused and complicated Delta political
and economic scene was made more so during the
1860s and 1870s. French traders began to invade the
Delta. The British who, as late as 1865, counseled a

policy of retreat from West Africa, were forced to
make an about-face. As the imperial race for African
territory heated up, culminating in the scramble for
all of Africa during the 1880s and 1890s, the European merchants joined together in quasi-national
trading companies. One such was the National African Company of Taubman Goldie (later Sir George
Taubman Goldie) which, in 1886, was chartered as
the Royal Niger Company. Goldie at first concentrated his operation almost exclusively in the Delta.
Between 1879 and 1884, he managed to squeeze the
French traders out of the Delta. His most immova-
ble opposition, however, came from a Delta chief
named Jaja.

Jaja was born in Iboland in 1821 and was sold as a
slave to the house of Anna Pepple in Bonny. He
eventually rose to head the house but, in 1870, Jaja
left Bonny and founded his own kingdom in Opobo.
Jaja was already well on his way to becoming the
most important and powerful ruler in the Delta.
After his blockade of Bonny brought the city-state
to its knees, ruining a number of English palm oil
exporters in the process, he achieved his coveted
aim. Jaja did not stop with the bankrupting of Bonny. He pressed on, extending his rule over many of
the territories bordering on Opobo. The British
merchants were greatly alarmed at this turn of
events. Their bargaining position had been weakened by Bonny's demise and Opobo's simultaneous
rise. Jaja had, by the early 1880s, all but cornered
the flow of palm oil from Iboland. The traders connected with the British port of Liverpool were par-

ticularly hard hit. Liverpool's wealth depended upon the palm oil trade in the nineteenth century as it had upon the slave trade in the seventeenth and eighteenth centuries. Now Jaja indicated that he preferred to barter with Glasgow, Liverpool's commercial rival.

Jaja's sway over the Delta region and the German annexation in 1884 of the Cameroons to the east, nearly wrecked Goldie's master plan for the acquisition of all of Nigeria. With the French advancing steadily from the northwest, Goldie was given the green light by the British government to acquire as much of Nigeria as possible through treaties with the Delta city-states and other coastal peoples. With few exceptions, the chiefs willingly signed these agreements, which placed their homelands under British "protection." Jaja was suspicious and initially resisted Goldie's overtures but, after receiving assurances that his trading rights would be respected, he, too, accepted British "protection" in 1884.

In November 1884, Europe's imperial powers met at Berlin to set the ground rules for the West African land grab. By that time, Goldie had succeeded in establishing, on paper at least, a British sphere, including Opobo, throughout most of lower Nigeria. In June 1885, Great Britain declared its Oil Rivers Protectorate over the region.

Jaja had, through his trading operation, continued to obstruct the freewheeling British merchants. In 1887, Goldie's personal guarantee notwithstanding, the British consul, Harry Johnson, urged on by the

Liverpool palm oil interests, lured Jaja aboard a British ship and spirited him off to Accra. Soon after, the Opobo king was deported to the West Indies where he died in 1891.

Jaja was not alone among Delta chiefs in opposing British imperialism in the Delta. Another was Nana Olumu, an Itsekiri king, who monopolized the palm oil trade in the Benin River, in opposition to the British policy of free trade. Like Jaja, he was an independent operator and as such was destined to share the same fate. In 1891, Nana, who the British had appointed Governor of the Benin River in 1884, found his empire enclosed within the Oil Rivers Protectorate. Three years later, a British patrol drove him from his headquarters at Ebrohimi. The wily Nana, who was not above trafficking in slaves, escaped, but later surrendered to the British and was exiled to Accra. He was permitted to return to his own country in 1906, and died in 1916.

While occasional rebellions, such as the burning in 1895 of the Royal Niger Company's Akassa trading post by Brass tribesmen, took place, the hold of the Delta city-states over the palm oil trade had effectively been broken with the fall of Jaja and Nana. The palm oil monopoly passed to the British Delta merchants. When, by 1906, the last vestiges of resistance in the Niger Delta and in the Ibo hinterland had been crushed, the undermining of the economic prosperity and political power of the city-states, begun under John Beecroft a half century earlier, was finally accomplished.

CHAPTER THREE

Europe, West Africa, and the Slave Trade

It is time for those who direct the councils of the nations to turn their eyes on the trade to Africa. This traffic in the human species, so direct and daring an infringement of every principle of liberty and justice, has attracted the public notice. The more it is examined, the more horrid it will appear; and the voice of reason, aided by the natural feelings of the human heart must sooner or later achieve its overthrow. — Dr. James Currie, a Scotch physician and abolitionist, in 1785[46]

IN MANY RESPECTS, the fifteenth and sixteenth centuries are rightly considered to be eras of exploration and expansion. With the improvement in navigational devices and ship construction, the European sailor could venture far beyond the lands visited by his predecessors. The bursting of the shell that enclosed Europe was all part of a wider struggle which saw the major European nations competing for superiority in trade, a contest that would propel the ships of Europe to the four points of the compass.

As a people whose livelihood depended upon the sea, it was almost predictable that the Portuguese would make the first intensive investigation of the West African coast. Nevertheless, there is evidence suggesting that the Norman seafarers of Dieppe on France's rocky Atlantic coast landed and settled at Elmina and Senegal in the fourteenth century, one hundred years before the Portuguese anchored off the same shore. But these depots had to be abandoned because France was involved in what came to be known as the Hundred Years' War and could ill-afford to support overseas adventures. As further proof of its contact with West Africa, the town of Dieppe is known for its ivory carvings, a skill born on Africa's west coast, where elephants roamed freely long ago.

Whoever was first, the Dieppois or the Portuguese, there certainly is little doubt that the Portuguese had the greatest initial impact on West Africa and its peoples. During the lifetime of Prince Henry the Navigator, the Portuguese captain Gil Eannes sailed beyond the forbidding Cape Bojador (the "bulging cape") in 1434. South of the cape it was said that the water boiled and a man's skin was blackened by the heat of the tropical sun. It is true that the shoals off Cape Bojador made sailing difficult, but the Portuguese surmounted the difficulties, and one more barrier separating Europe and West Africa was removed. It must be remembered that the Portuguese were, by the fifteenth century, familiar with Africa and its inhabitants. The caravans that crisscrossed North Africa and the Sahara brought with them, in addition to spices, cotton, ivory, and gold, colorful tales of African civilizations and kingdoms. The Catalan Atlas, written by a Mallorcan Jew in 1375, depicted Mali, Gao, and Timbuktu, as the sources from whence the gold, slaves, and spices came and remarked on the vast empire of Mansa Musa. After Gil Eannes, other Portuguese mariners tried their luck. Nuno Tristão, in 1443, reached Arguin Island which, within two years, would become the first European slave station. Curiously enough, Tristao was later killed by African tribesmen who had been told by Muslim informants that Christians were cannibals.

On one of these voyages, slaves were purchased and presented as a gift to Prince Henry. Africa thus suffered its first taste of what was to become a commonplace occurrence over the next four hundred years. Slavery, of course, was well established in Africa long before the Europeans arrived. But African slavery was on a scale that would later be dwarfed by the European appetite for booty and riches.

After Prince Henry's death in 1460, the Portuguese moved farther down the coast—as far as the Bight of Benin—and inland to Tekrur and, some think, Timbuktu. John II, who reigned in Portugal from 1481 to 1495, showed an avid interest in West Africa and ordered the founding of a trading depot on the Gold Coast:

> The king [of Portugal], considering, as a wise man, the great profit and good health which his subjects would

receive in body and soul . . . if he were to possess in those parts of Mina [Elmina] a fortress of his own. . . . For this purpose, he ordered that all the timber and free-stones, which would be necessary . . . should forthwith be cut and shaped in this country, so that without any delay in the work they could be set in place immediately.[47]

While the West African coast was considered a prize by Portugal's royal court, and a monopoly was declared over its gold and trade in slaves, it excited less attention than Vasco da Gama's pioneering voyage to India in 1497. In 1500, the market for slaves remained small while India, with her jewels and spices, beckoned with the promise of untold riches.

However, as the Spanish colonies in the Americas grew, and the native Indians proved unsuited to the unbearable tasks required of them in mining and plantation work, the slave trade increased.

Portugal's sovereignty over the West African coast was seriously contested at the end of the sixteenth century with the appearance of the Dutch in West African waters. In the face of this stiff competition, Portugal's weaknesses became all the more glaring. In 1580, Portugal had been incorporated into the Spanish empire and the products of Asia and Africa, carried in Portuguese ships, were now unavailable to the Dutch. The only alternative for the Dutch was to go directly to the source. In Amsterdam, the Dutch East India Company and the Dutch West India Company were formed and the lines of conflict were thus clearly drawn.

Most of the slave trade was conducted in Portuguese vessels on contract, or *Asiento*, to the Spanish crown. As the traffic burgeoned, the Portuguese sought to restrict the other European nations — Holland and England in particular — from entering what they considered their exclusive domain — the West African coast.

In 1596, the Dutch undertook a campaign against Portugal's hegemony over the West African coast. An attack on São Jorge da Mina, Portugal's Gold Coast fort, failed but the Dutch, undaunted, pecked away steadily, for the traffic in slaves was too lucrative for any trading nation to ignore.

The slave trade itself was only part of a grander design which became more apparent as Europe's overseas exploration increased. The Spanish flag flew over much of the Caribbean, South America, and parts of North America, territories that had been reserved to them by the 1493 papal Bull of Partition, but the other seagoing European nations were close on their heels. In 1609 Bermuda was claimed by the English, followed by St. Christopher (St. Kitts) in 1624 and the Barbadoes in 1625. The sugar island of Jamaica, captured from the Spanish, was annexed in 1650. The French took Guadeloupe in 1626 and Martinique nine years later. The Dutch had settled St. Eustasius, Tobago, and Curacao by the 1630s and had occupied part of Brazil. The Danes, in 1671, brought St. Thomas within their sphere. And, of course, on the North American continent, the struggle for empire was underway. The foothold gained by Europe in the Western Hemisphere made the slave trade necessary for colonial survival and abruptly ended Spanish and Portuguese plans for a trading monopoly.

For Portugal, the death blow to her supremacy over the West African coast fell in 1642 when the Dutch seized her Gold Coast fort of Axim, as well as Arguin, Goree, São Tomé, and Luanda. The toppling of the Portuguese and the ascendancy of the Dutch marked the beginning of a new phase in the struggle for strategic superiority in world trade.

It is worthwhile at this point to glance at the West African sources from which the slaves were exported. For convenience, the West African coast can be divided, as it was on seventeenth-century maps, into two regions: Upper Guinea, from Cabo Blanco to the eastern reaches of Sierra Leone, and Lower Guinea, which extends from there to the Cameroons. The coastline from northwest to southeast is about two thousand miles in length.

Though in the area of modern Guinea and Sierra Leone (then Upper Guinea) many slaves were captured and exported to the Caribbean sugar plantations, it was in Lower Guinea that the slave trade bloomed.

Lower Guinea can be split into four sections: the Grain Coast, the Ivory Coast, the Gold Coast, and the Slave Coast. The Grain Coast, which corresponds to Liberia, is a stretch of land washed by a heavy surf. It was from here that pepper and rice were brought to waiting ships in swift canoes manned by West Africa's preeminent seamen, the

Kru. The Krumen, who served in many trading capacities along the coast, also ferried slaves, some of whom were taken in the Grain Coast's hinterland.

The Ivory Coast during the seventeenth century was also known as the Tooth Coast. It was from the Ivory Coast that much of the ivory shipped to Europe originated. Unfortunately, the demand far exceeded the supply and, by the seventeenth century, the Ivory Coast's elephant herds had disappeared.

East of the Ivory Coast was the heavily populated Gold Coast, where European activity was centered. Along this coastal strip traders constructed commercial "forts" or "factories." It should be noted that the land on which these depots were situated was leased from West African kings. Many of these rulers were so powerful that the traders dared not tangle with them for fear of being expelled from the coast. The whole process of exchange was regulated by the African monarchs, many of whom profited greatly by selling their hapless subjects to the Europeans. The major slave suppliers were in fact the Ashanti, the Dahomeans, the Oyos, and the Bini of Benin. On occasion, when it appeared that the Europeans were threatening his authority, an African emperor might conduct a raid on one of the coastal depots. These forays increased during the eighteenth and nineteenth centuries when the Europeans penetrated farther inland.

During the slave trade's peak years in the seventeenth and eighteenth centuries, the British, French, Dutch, Danes, Portuguese, Swedes, and Brandenburg Germans together maintained a total of fifty factories or "castles" in the Gold Coast region. As the fortunes of each nation rose and fell, these depots would change hands. It was from them that slaves or gold from the hills and streams in the district were purchased from African middlemen. In return, the Europeans offered textiles, mostly woven in India, English cutlery and firearms in growing quantities, watered-down spirits, iron and brass which the Africans would shape into tools, basins, and assorted other commodities.

The slaves — usually males aged 10 to 35 — were kept in barracoons, or slave houses, where they were inspected by the ship's surgeon and branded with the initials of their buyer. They were then rowed by Krumen to the slaver for the six- to ten-week voyage across the Atlantic. In the stinking holds where the slaves were chained, they were subjected to bad food, disease, and the brutality of the crew. More than sixteen percent of the slaves usually died in transit, and often the figure ran much higher. It is one of the ironies of the slave trade that large numbers of seamen perished, too. In extreme cases, whole cargoes of slaves were lost, but this was rare. A slave was valuable property and theoretically, at least, had to be protected from abuse which could damage him and render him useless. While the horrors of the infamous "Middle Passage" to the Americas were shocking, each captain was responsible for delivering as many slaves as possible. If he lost too many, he would face certain bankruptcy.

After the Gold Coast came the Slave Coast, east of the Volta River, from which many Yoruba, Dahomean, and Ibo slaves were sent. In the Gold Coast and Slave Coast, with its many tributaries, lagoons, and swamps, the slave trade was most difficult to eradicate and continued well after its abolition by most of the European nations.

By the time the Dutch had acquired Axim, the West Indian sugar, coffee, tobacco, and indigo plantations were in full operation and their crops in great demand throughout Europe. To fill this demand, the planted acreage was increased. More slaves were brought to the New World to work the land. For a time, Dutch power was at its zenith, and Europe's goods were carried in the holds of their ships, but the English and French soon challenged their lead. England had been trading in slaves since the 1530s when William Hawkins made his way around Cape Bojador and returned home with a hull filled with ivory and a few slaves. His son, John Hawkins, sponsored by a London corporation, took three ships to West Africa in 1562 with the sole purpose of slaving. With the voyage of John Hawkins, the British slave trade was thus begun in earnest. The French, too, entered the slave trading field along with the Swedes, the Danes, and the Brandenburgers in the sixteenth century.

To finance their operations, each nation organized a national trading monopoly that licensed individual traders. In 1660, the Company of Royal Adventurers Trading to Africa was chartered in England. In 1672, it was succeeded by the Royal African Company. The French West Indies Company was organized by Louis XIV's chief minister, Jean-Baptiste Colbert, in 1664. By 1702, it had captured the coveted *Asiento*, the right to supply slaves to the Spanish colonies. The Swedes, Danes, and Germans also created national slave trading monopolies. In addition, the Dutch West India Company now had to contend with Dutch interlopers who sailed under foreign flags and the Dutch company's dominance of the slave trade was soon a thing of the past.

The most effective and successful of the trading companies was unquestionably the Royal African Company. It had, reportedly, carried five thousand slaves a year in the ships under its command before its charter was terminated in 1697 and its trade monopoly lifted.

After the War of Spanish Succession in 1713, the *Asiento* was transferred to Great Britain. With this and a growing merchant marine, England was able to carry the great bulk of the slave trade. The profits from the traffic contributed a broad stream of capital that later financed its Industrial Revolution.

By the eighteenth century, the slave trade was recognized as one leg of a larger, triangular trade. Ships built in England and Colonial America carried England's products to West Africa where they were bartered for slaves. The slaves would then be exported to the West Indies, South America, and the American colonies where they would then be exchanged for raw material—sugar, tobacco, indigo,

lumber, and cotton—which would then be brought
back to England. This was the direction of the cycle,
supplemented occasionally by a two-way trade between England and her colonies. It was this trade
which injected life into England's economy.

In countries such as Holland and England, where
individuals had so recently fought and died for religious and economic freedom, it seems surprising
that few voices were raised against the inhuman
traffic. But it must be noted that the English government was devoted to increasing England's wealth. In
an atmosphere where many became rich and powerful through the slave trade, few cried out in behalf
of the enslaved African and against the inhumanity
of trafficking in human beings. Yet there did arise in
England an anti-slavery movement which eventually
drew support from every strata of British society. It
was the English who profited most from the slave
trade but, paradoxically, it was the English who finally put an end to it.

The eighteenth century was a time of expansion
and concentrated wealth, but also an era of enlightenment. There is little doubt that the anti-slavery
impulse sprang from humanitarian ideals which had
permeated European thought during the century. As
early as 1696, a novelist, Mrs. Aphra Behn, described slavery's horrors in her novel, *Oroonoko*.
Daniel Defoe, the author of *Robinson Crusoe*, condemned the slave trade in *The Reformation of Manners* in 1702.

However, until the English Quakers made known

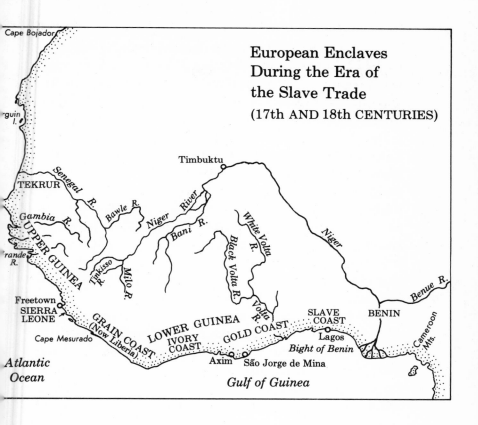

European Enclaves
During the Era of
the Slave Trade
(17th AND 18th CENTURIES)

their opposition to the slave trade in 1729, no group
had taken a firm stand against it. The first genuine
blow against the institution of slavery and the practice of slaving was struck by Granville Sharp, later
the sponsor of Sierra Leone. Sharp had given refuge
to an abandoned slave named Jonathan Strong. The
slave's master subsequently sued to have Strong returned. Quite unexpectedly, Strong was freed by the
court.

No decision on slavery's legality was reached until 1772 in the Somerset case. The slave, Somerset, was brought from Virginia to England by his owner and then escaped. He was captured and sent to Jamaica for sale. In an effort to settle the issue out of court, England's Chief Justice, Lord Mansfield, advised both parties to the suit to seek a compromise. Mansfield's suggestion was disregarded and the judge was forced to hand down a decision. He ordered Somerset freed. Another decision rendered in the 1778 Knight case stated that "the defender [slave owner] had no right to the negro's service at any time." Following the settlement of both the Somerset and Knight cases, slavery, in England and Scotland at least, was abolished.

The problem of the slave trade, unfortunately, was still to be solved. Benjamin Franklin aptly commented upon "the hypocrisy of the country [England] which encourages such a detestable commerce by laws for promoting the Guinea [slave] trade; while it piques itself on its virtue, love of liberty, and the equity of its courts in setting free a single negro." Franklin's charge had the loud ring of truth to it but he conveniently ignored the fact that his own American compatriots bloodied their hands by engaging in the slave trade, also. It would be another thirty years before the slave trade, the mainspring of the slave system, was officially abolished.

In the early 1780s, the first abolition motion was introduced into the House of Commons. It urged that the traffic be abolished because "the slave trade

is contrary to the laws of God and the rights of
Man." It was soundly defeated. The fear of economic
disaster was widespread, especially in Liverpool, the
port that benefited most from the slave trade and in
which feeling ran highest against abolition. One
example of the exaggerated importance assigned to
the slave trade is indicated by this election broad-
side:

> *If our slave trade had gone there's an*
> * end to our lives*
> *Beggars all we must be, our children*
> * and wives*
> *No ships from our ports, their proud*
> * sails e'er would spread*
> *And our streets grown with grass where*
> * the cows might be fed.*[48]

In 1787, the year in which the first of England's
liberated blacks were sent to Sierra Leone, English
abolitionist activity came into sharp focus. From
1787 until 1807, when the slave trade was made illegal, the London Committee for the Abolition of
the Slave Trade provided the impetus for the abolition movement. Under the leadership of Granville
Sharp, Thomas Clarkson, William Wilberforce, William Pitt, and Charles James Fox, the London Committee pressed toward its ultimate goal.

While humane reasons were offered for abolition,
the London Committee wisely stressed the alternatives of legitimate commerce. The economic approach turned out to be one of the most powerful
arguments in favor of abolition. The abolitionists

emphasized the fact that for centuries England had conducted a viable trade in pepper, palm oil, and other products with West Africa. Pressure against the slave trade was increased in Parliament. While abolition measures were consistently defeated, at least the horrors of the trade were kept in the public eye. In 1792, a sugar boycott was organized by Thomas Clarkson. One of the pamphlets distributed in favor of the boycott asserted that "every person who habitually consumes one article of West Indian produce, raised by slaves, is guilty of the crime of murder."

But the slave trade continued and the London Committee's effectiveness reached a low point when Napoleon came to power in France. The Napoleonic Wars consumed England's energies and preoccupied Parliament. It had been hoped that before the war's outbreak, France, too, would abolish the slave trade. The French had their own abolitionist circle, the *Societé des Amis des Noirs* (among whose members were included a hero of the American Revolution, the Marquis de Lafayette, the philosopher Condorcet, and the revolutionary, Honoré Mirabeau), which campaigned against the slave trade. Unfortunately, the war ended the chances for mutual abolition.

The Napoleonic Wars also changed the atmosphere in Parliament. Any attack on the Establishment, of which the business of slaving was a part, was looked upon with a jaundiced eye. The pro-slave trade people seized upon Wilberforce's being made an honorary French citizen by the Revolutionary Convention and Clarkson's seeking the support of the French revolutionist, Honoré Mirabeau, as evidence that the abolitionists were fomentors of revolution. The anti-French hysteria that gripped England severely weakened the abolitionist movement. The prospects for abolition were dim in this period of uncertainty as Napoleon's armies trampled over Europe and the French navy, which burned Freetown in Sierra Leone to the ground in 1794, vied with Great Britain for control of the seas.

Along the Gold and Slave Coasts, Africans were still being torn from their homes, separated from their families, and sold to the highest bidder.

In 1804, in the face of renewed international warfare, the abolitionists, led by Wilberforce, Fox, and Pitt, vowed to continue the fight. They could point to Denmark's abolition of the slave trade in 1803 as a precedent. Wilberforce could cite the rebellions that had flared up in the West Indies. In French-held Haiti, slaves led by Toussaint L'Ouverture had crushed their European overlords. In Jamaica, the Maroons, runaway slaves of Ashanti origin, had established a mountain stronghold and only concerted government efforts dislodged them. The importation of more slaves, the abolitionists argued, would foster more revolts and could ultimately ruin the West Indies' precious sugar economy.

In 1806, the abolitionists suffered a setback when two of their most valued and articulate supporters,

William Pitt and Charles James Fox, died. It was left
to William Wilberforce to lead the battle against
the slave trade in the House of Commons. In the
House of Lords, many churchmen threw their support to abolition. Wilberforce's persistence at last
began to pay dividends. Backing for abolition had
increased substantially during the three years from
1804 to 1807. The margin of defeat for each succeeding abolition bill grew smaller. Yet there was a
disquieting development brewing in government
circles. The administration of Lord William Grenville, sympathetic to abolition, was in political trouble over an issue that placed it at odds with the English king, George III. Its time was fast running out.
Wilberforce was aware that if the latest abolition
measure failed in the current Parliamentary session,
it might be postponed indefinitely. A new ministry
would likely have in it members hostile to abolition. The measure fortunately was passed by both
houses of Parliament at almost the last moment.
Lord Grenville, as ecstatic as Wilberforce over the
outcome of the vote, congratulated Parliament for
"having performed one of the most glorious acts
that had ever been done by any assembly of any nation in the world."

A desperate attempt to stave off the inevitable
was staged by the Society of West Indian Merchants
and Planters who petitioned King George III, im-
ploring him "to avert the approaching destruction of
their fellow subjects who are inhabitants of these
colonies," and withhold his signature from the abo-

lition bill. Their pleas were of no avail. On March 25, 1807, the king signed the measure. Later that day, the Grenville government was dissolved, the abolition bill its last and only memorable act.

The new law decreed that after January 1, 1808, "all manner of dealing and trading in slaves in Africa, or in their transport from Africa to any place," was to be "utterly abolished, prohibited and declared to be unlawful." Liverpool's overall trade suffered at first but it was not long before she had recovered fully. As Wilberforce and the abolitionists had predicted, Liverpool became in time England's leading importer of West Africa's agricultural products. This trade was based on palm oil, mainly from the former slave source, the Niger Delta.

But an extensive legitimate trade was still some way off. The chorus of bravos for the abolition act came too soon. There were always slave smugglers who gambled against capture, for the rewards for violating the slave trading prohibition were high. Groups were formed to outfit ships in European ports. Even in Liverpool and London, illegal ship outfitting took place. Slaves were still in demand in Brazil, the United States (which had abolished the slave trade in 1808), and Cuba. Fortunes could still be made. Despite the enactment of additional laws, some providing the death penalty for slaving, the slave trade was revived.

Great Britain, in 1815, brought the issue of slave trading before the Congress of Vienna which, while it heartily condemned slaving, did nothing to enforce its abolition. Great Britain succeeded in concluding abolition treaties with Sweden, Denmark, Holland, and Spain by 1820 but the slave trade still continued. Clearly, it remained a profitable business and the fear that its abolition would affect the lucrative sugar market prevailed. The Portuguese, who agreed to stop slave trading north of the Equator, proceeded south of the line to depopulate the Congo and Angola coasts, exporting captives to the plantations of Brazil and Cuba.

Almost alone, Great Britain sought to implement the ban. In 1811, the British navy could spare only five ships for anti-slaving duty along the West African coast, and the seamen who manned the vessels had often been forced to serve. Until the British navy instituted reforms in 1836, the character and morale of the squadron's members were relatively low. Service in the British navy was itself a form of servitude for many sailors. From Freetown harbor in Sierra Leone, the West African Squadron was expected to patrol the two thousand miles of coastline, from Cape Mesurado to Lagos in the Niger Delta, an almost impossible assignment. The coast was broken by rivers, lagoons, swamps, and creeks, each a potential hiding place from which Africans could be put aboard clandestine slavers. If a slave ship was captured, the captain and its crew would be brought to Freetown where they would stand trial. The slaves would then be set free in Sierra Leone or, in the case of a slaver captured by an American cruiser, in Liberia.

The abolition of the slave trade was only the first step. The abolitionists, under the leadership of Thomas Fowell Buxton, now turned their attention to the principal evil—slavery itself. While it had been prohibited in England and Scotland since the 1770s, elsewhere in its empire, in the United States, and in Cuba and Brazil, slavery was still a fact.

Slavery's defenses had been breached with the abolition of slave trafficking but not until 1833 was slavery in the British empire (outside of England and Scotland) outlawed. For a period of five years following liberation, the ex-slaves were required to serve an apprenticeship to ease the economic blow to the West Indian sugar planters. In 1838, abolition was completed in England's overseas possessions.

Meanwhile, along the West African coast, more ships had been added to the British squadron, fast sloops that made great headway against the illegal trade. Where they could, British residents, especially in Sierra Leone, worked toward suppressing the traffic in their domains. Unfortunately, many of the treaties made with African chiefs for the purpose of ending the slave trade were rejected by Parliament. It feared the extension of British influence and involvement into areas that it could not control. Not until 1861, with the annexation of Lagos, was this patchwork of agreements completed and slaving inhibited at its source.

It remained obvious that only the expansion of legitimate trade and the constriction of the slave markets could effectively destroy the slave trade.

Fortunately, the trade in palm oil, ground nuts, and pepper, exported from the Niger Delta, grew steadily. Yet slaves, too, were still being transshipped to the United States, Cuban, and Brazilian markets.

To discuss slavery in the United States and its effect on the millions kept in bondage, oppressed, violated, and murdered, is a formidable task and cannot be undertaken in a few short paragraphs. It was recognized as an unquestionable evil by many but, like the slave trade in England and slavery in the West Indies, it was also an integral part of the American economy. As in England, brave men, both black and white, came forth, and soon a river of opposition flowed against what has been called our "peculiar institution." But, in the United States, the Southern "slavocracy," with its dependence upon the cotton crop, carried far more political weight with its government than did the West Indians and slave traders with theirs. Cotton was king in America's South, a monarch difficult to dethrone. The issue of slavery could not be settled without a civil war, so devastating that it ripped the nation asunder and from which the nation has yet to recover. When the shooting stopped in 1865, America's black slaves had been legally emancipated. The biggest market for slaves was now closed forever. The British annexation of Lagos in 1861, from which many slaves had been slipped past the British coastal patrol, drove another nail into the slave trade's coffin. The end of Cuban slavery, decreed in 1869, and its abolition in Brazil soon thereafter, sounded the death knell for the slave trade. The traffic in human souls, begun over four centuries earlier at the cost of millions of lives, would no longer bring undeserved profits to those who built their wealth upon human suffering.

Various estimates have been offered as to the number of slaves transported from West Africa from 1500 to the late nineteenth century. One sets the figure at 20 millions, another at 15 millions. The most detailed analysis, however, has been made by Professor Philip Curtin. Researching shipping records and taking into account shipping resources available at the time, he has concluded that the number of slaves landed in the Americas and Europe probably did not exceed 9.5 millions. Curtin's data also suggest that the mortality rate among slaves was roughly sixteen percent which indicates that the slaves exported from West Africa totaled slightly more than 11 millions. Until the European nations abolished the trade, most slaves were sent from the Gold Coast and Slave Coast. After abolition, and when the policing of West Africa's waters by the British began to bring results, the slave hunters preyed farther north, particularly along the so-called Grain Coast.

The unadorned numbers, while they place the slave trade in perspective, cannot convey the effect slaving has had upon West Africa. The cost to West Africa in manpower was great if one considers that only the young and healthy were enslaved, leaving behind the old and infirm, thus retarding population growth. The slave trade did draw political power from the Western Sudan to the coast and it did bring to West Africa such staple crops as sugar, yams, and corn from the Americas in return. But, more important, it destroyed many defenseless peoples who were the object of predatory raids aimed at filling the demand for plantation labor. Native crafts and skills were wiped out. The disappearance of brass casting, ivory carving, and cloth weaving serve to prove this point.

West African development may not have been halted but it was surely slowed and redirected to serve other, alien, needs after the Europeans landed. The benefits of the European life style were imported but this surely cannot erase the destruction wrought by the slave trade nor does it balance what West Africa lost in the process.

1 Standing bronze figure of a hornblower.
Benin, circa 16th century. (Courtesy, The
Museum of Primitive Art, New York)

2   A horseman of the Western Sudan,
sketched by Major Dixon Denham, 1826.

3   A parade in Benin during the seventeenth century

4 A village in Niger.

5 The Sultan of Bornu prepares to receive
the Denham-Clapperton-Oudney mission, 1825.

6 The ancient gates of Kano (Nigeria).
(Photograph from Nigerian Information Services)

7 These are some of the emblems adopted by the Dahomean kings to symbolize their regal power. King Behanzin, who reigned from 1889 to 1894, chose a shark as his emblem.

8　Elmina Castle, built by the Portuguese in 1482, was later the headquarters of the British in the Gold Coast for many years.

9　A Senufo mask, The Ivory Coast.
(Courtesy, The Museum of Primitive Art, New York)

11   Mungo Park (1771-1806), explorer of the Niger.

10   Agaja, King of Dahomey, reigned from 1708 to 1740.

12   The nineteenth-century Dahomean kings, Gelele and Gezo.

13 Slaves on the deck of the captured slave ship,
Wildfire, being brought into Key West,
April 30, 1860.

14 Al Kanemi, the Sultan
of Bornu (1808-1835).

15 James Africanus Beale Horton (1835-1882), the Sierra-Leonean-born physician and African nationalist.

16 Dr. Edward Wilmot Blyden (1832-1912), nine-teenth-century West Indian-born Liberian statesman and black nationalist.

17 Dr. W. E. B. DuBois
(Photograph reproduced by permission of The Crisis and N.A.A.C.P.)

18 Marcus Garvey (1887-1940), Jamaican-born founder of the Universal Negro Improvement Association and spokesman for the "Back to Africa" movement.

19 A Cameroonian casting his ballot during the Northern Cameroons Plebiscite, November 1959.

20 A rubber plantation in Western Nigeria. (Courtesy Nigerian Information Services)

21 Sékou Touré of Guinea, Modibo Keita of Mali, and Kwame
Nkrumah of Ghana at a meeting of the Ghana-Guinea-Mali Union
in 1961. (Wide World Photos)

22 An Ibibio mask, Nigeria.
(Courtesy, The Museum of Primitive Art, New York)

3 A traditional dance performed by Nigerian students.
(Courtesy Nigerian Information Services)

24 Dr. K. A. Busia, the Ghanaian Prime Minister, being
sworn into office at the State House in Accra, October 1969.

25 The mosque in Bobo-Dioulasso, Upper Volta.

26 Agni funerary figure, The Ivory Coast.
(Courtesy, The Museum of Primitive Art, New York)

CHAPTER FOUR

Freedom's Enclaves: Sierra Leone and Liberia

SIERRA LEONE

The Portugals in these parts lived liker Ethnikes than Christians. The king of Sierra Leone had timber cut for a church, and was wonderfull desirous of Baptisme. The king was named Philip and is called Philip Leonis. . . . This countrey is as healthfull as any I ever came in, and Sierra Leone would be a fit place for a plantation of the Society [of Jesus].—BARREIRO, a Portuguese Jesuit, 1605.[49]

THE PORTUGUESE EXPLORER, Pedro da Cintra, has been credited with giving the name Serra Lyoa, or Lion Mountain, to the landfall he observed in 1462 while sailing along that part of the West African coast we know today as Sierra Leone. In the sixteenth century, Valentim Fernandes, a German printer living in Lisbon, wrote of the settlements that dotted this coast. He described the structure of the mud huts and the brick buildings that served the richer tribesmen as homes, and also described the forms of government found in these villages.

These indigenous Sierra Leonean civilizations

107

soon had a taste of European civilization at its worst when John Hawkins and his slaving expedition arrived in 1562. Richard Hakluyt, the sixteenth-century chronicler of England's overseas adventures, recorded the event:

> From [Tenerife, Hawkins] passed to Sierra Leona, upon the coast of Guinea, which place by the people of the countrey is called Tagarin, where he stayed some good time, and got into his possession, partly by the sworde, and partly by other means, to the number of 300 Negros at the least, besides other merchandises which that countrey yeeldeth.[50]

Initially, the native Bulom and Temne tribes cordially greeted the Europeans who supplied them with firearms and other European products including, according to the British captain William Towerson, who touched at Sierra Leone in 1556, "basons, pots of course tinne, wedges of yron, blew corall, horse tailes, kettles of Dutchland, great brasse buttons, great knives of a low price, great pinnes, &c."

But it soon became evident to the Sierra Leoneans that the Europeans had a greater need for slaves than they did for the ivory from the dense forests of Guinea or the gold of the Western Sudan. At first, few were taken, for the sugar plantations of the West Indies had yet to firmly establish themselves. But, by the seventeenth century, the slave trade had become a thriving business and, during the next two centuries, as we have already noted, slave raiding and trading increased sharply.

In the midst of this vicious traffic were the Sierra

Leone tribes who suffered almost as much as their neighbors to the east. In the seventeenth century, many settlements were destroyed and the famous Bulom ivory carvers disappeared, yet another victim of Europe's intrusion into West Africa.

However, the horizon brightened for West Africa's coastal peoples during the intellectual enlightenment which marked the eighteenth century. The plight of human beings everywhere, in Africa as well as in Europe, became the object of widespread popular concern. In 1778, slavery in Great Britain was outlawed, a momentous act which resulted in the emancipation of more than 15,000 slaves. Yet the joy over receiving the precious gift of freedom was tempered by the fact that England's Black Poor, as they were known, had few trades or skills with which to support themselves. Freed from bondage, they streamed into England's cities in search of work. But, as for the unskilled throughout history, there were few jobs available and a social crisis of some magnitude was created. Following the American Revolution, the situation worsened when the slaves who remained with the Loyalists during the war swelled the ranks of the Black Poor.

The idea of resettling freed slaves in Africa became increasingly popular during the last quarter of the eighteenth century. A society for resettlement was chartered in 1779 by the Swedish king Gustavus III. It provided for the settlement of forty families. The English movement had its real beginnings after a British naturalist, Dr. Henry Smeatham, returned

to England from a residence in Sierra Leone. Dr.
Smeatham suggested to the noted abolitionist Granville Sharp the returning of the Black Poor to Sierra
Leone "for the purpose of checking and putting
down the slave-trade, and of diffusing the Christian
religion among the natives." Sharp was intrigued by
the idea and, with the sponsorship of missionary
societies and the African Association, organized
support for a colony of freed slaves. Sierra Leone
was chosen for the experiment and land was "purchased" from the Temne chief, King Tom, and the
senior chief, King Naimbana for a small amount of
cloth, arms, tobacco, and rum. It was on this twenty-
square-mile patch, fondly called the Province of
Freedom by Sharp, that some four hundred black
and a smattering of white settlers arrived in May
1787. On May 14, the Union Jack was raised and the
settlement of Granville Town was created. Yet the
first effort to found a colony in Sierra Leone was
doomed to failure. Fever and conflict with the native
tribesmen reduced the number of settlers and, despite the arrival of a relief ship in 1788, the population continued to decline. In 1789, King Tom's successor, King Jimmy, after a dispute with a British
agent over the slave trade, attacked Granville Town,
drove out the settlers, and burned it to the ground.
The first colonization attempt ended in disaster.
Whether it would have survived under any circumstances was questionable. The black settlers were a
Europeanized group, unsuited to the climate and the
assorted environmental problems with which they

had to contend in the land of their forebears. In their strange new home, it was increasingly difficult to acclimate themselves. The demise of the Province of Freedom was perhaps a foregone conclusion, but the optimism of Granville Sharp and his fellow abolitionist, Thomas Clarkson, was not dampened.

Sharp was determined to make the Province of Freedom work. In 1790, the St. George's Bay Association was formed and a charter was requested "to colonize a small part of the coast of Africa to introduce civilization among the natives, and to cultivate the soil by means of free labor." The aim of Sierra Leone's sponsors was now to organize a company that would promote legitimate trade with Sierra Leone's interior and use the earnings from this trade to support the colony. In 1791, the St. George's Bay Association became the Sierra Leone Company. From its beginning, it was clear that white Europeans rather than black would govern Sierra Leone. A governor assisted by a council of eight advisors was chosen by the directors of the London-based corporation and was responsible to the company, not to Sierra Leone's black settlers. As the settlement's population increased, the division between its people and their paternalistic government widened.

In March 1792, 1,200 freed slaves under the command of Thomas Peters, a black Loyalist and ex-sergeant in the British army, debarked at Granville Town, now renamed Freetown. This was the end of Thomas Peters' long journey, which had taken him to England in 1791 as the spokesman for the disillu-

sioned blacks who had fought with the British during the American Revolution. For their services,
they had been promised freedom and tracts of land
in Nova Scotia. When they arrived to take posses-
sion of their allotments, they found them to be
rocky and practically untillable.

While he was in London, Peters' case was taken
up by Thomas Clarkson, who secured passage and
land for the Nova Scotians in Sierra Leone. Soon
after setting foot in Freetown, they found themselves in conflict with the Sierra Leone administration. The dispute was over quit rents for the land
Clarkson assured them they would be granted
free. This issue was not resolved before Thomas
Peters, disappointed and depressed, died in 1792,
his Nova Scotian contingent betrayed once more by
the British.

Within two years, Sierra Leone was confronted
with another crisis. The volatile European situation
had erupted and France and Great Britain found
themselves on opposite sides. In 1794, a French
naval squadron entered Freetown harbor, bombard-
ed the town, and then sacked it. This shock was followed by an outbreak of disease which rocked the
already shaky colony even further.

One of the few bright spots during this decade
was the judicious leadership of the new governor,
Zachary Macaulay (1794–1799). Macaulay temporarily cooled the tempers of the black colonists
when he extended to them a small voice in running
the affairs of Sierra Leone. Unfortunately, Macau-

lay's successor, Thomas Ludlam, lacked the diplomatic skill and ability to deal equitably with the
Nova Scotian and Poor Black settlers. In 1800, he
was faced with a dual revolt, one by the Temne tribe
over land rights, the other by the Nova Scotians
who demanded more than token representation in
the government. Once again, the colony's future
looked bleak. It survived on a hand-to-mouth basis,
it was troubled internally, and its white leadership
was less than exceptionally qualified. Ludlam realized that without Nova Scotian backing the colony
would never achieve stability, much less prosperity.
In addition, the antipathy of the Temne tribe affected the colony's efforts to open Sierra Leone's interi-
or to trade.

In 1800, a new element was introduced into the
colony's complex state of affairs with the arrival of
the Maroons from the Caribbean sugar island of
Jamaica. In the early seventeenth century, these
people of Ashanti origin escaped from the sugar
plantations and hid in the mountains where they
created their own nation. Efforts by the Jamaican
government to recapture them failed. The Maroons
clung to their hard-won and valiantly defended freedom until the Jamaican army used packs of trained
and vicious dogs against them. Unable to cope with
this new tactic, the Maroons were overcome. The
Jamaican governor, however, realized that the Maroons could never be reintegrated into Jamaica's
slave society. Arrangements were therefore made to
deport the Maroons to Sierra Leone.

In September 1800, 550 Maroons landed at Freetown. Ignorant of the background which had precipitated the conflict with the Nova Scotians, the
Maroons sided with Governor Ludlam. The Nova
Scotians were placed at a serious disadvantage and
their only recourse was to retreat.

The problems with the Temne, too, were far from
solved. In 1801 and 1802, they attacked Freetown
and only the presence of British sailors saved the
colony from the same fate it had suffered at French
hands in 1794. In 1803, another Temne raid was
staged, but this too was halted. The Temne, defeated
and dispossessed, finally signed a peace treaty with
the Sierra Leone government in 1807.

By this time, the colony was at the point of economic ruin. Her chronically weak economy barely
survived the French razing of Freetown, the Nova
Scotian hostility, and the Temne uprisings. Farmers
abandoned their land to seek work in Freetown, and
the few skilled settlers had dwindled to less than
one hundred. In 1806, the directors of the Sierra
Leone Company considered the situation hopeless
and requested the transfer of the colony to the British government. In 1808, Sierra Leone became a
British Crown Colony. If its resources promised no
great economic returns, Freetown provided at least a
good harbor from which the Royal Navy could patrol the coast and enforce the newly passed British
law against slave trading.

The year 1808 began a new era for Sierra Leone.
The Royal Navy began to capture a sizeable number

of slavers, returning their liberated human cargoes to Freetown. In 1815, it was estimated that more than 6,000 recaptives (70,000 had been freed by 1850) had been repatriated in Sierra Leone. These liberated Africans, whose children came to be known as Creoles, would one day play an active part in the political and economic activities of the colony. Some sought careers in the army; others became traders. This caused friction between them and the older, more settled Sierra Leonean merchants. Riots and fights were frequent but, despite the impossible odds, the recaptives, especially the women among them, prospered. A number of recaptives and their families opted for return to the West African interior. A group of recaptives were among the founders of the Nigerian city of Abeokuta. Elsewhere along the coast their influence was felt and their talent used to create towns and trading centers.

The missionary societies of England, fervent supporters of abolition and the Sierra Leone project, saw in the recaptives a wealthy source of converts. Many recaptives and Creoles did, in fact, adopt Christianity. Quite a few rose to positions of importance within their respective religious orders.

In 1816, the march of Christianity in Africa found a reliable ally in Sierra Leone's acting governor, Sir Charles MacCarthy. Like many of his contemporaries in nineteenth-century British-ruled Africa (General Charles George Gordon in East Africa was another example) MacCarthy was part religious visionary. He viewed his role in Sierra Leone as a mandate for making the colony a center of Christianity.

In 1827, the Church Missionary Society established the Fourah Bay Training Institution for religious education. In the early nineteenth century, the British Parliament, through its special Liberated African Department, supplied a grant to assist the missionary schools and churches in Sierra Leone. By 1845, education in the colony was turned over exclusively to the missions. (In 1845, the Fourah Bay Training Institution became Fourah Bay College and its curriculum was broadened to include nonreligious subjects.)

Part of MacCarthy's dream had been to eliminate the slave trade. By negotiating treaties with local chiefs, the governor proceeded with his personal plan for Africa's salvation. Parliament wanted no part of MacCarthy's scheme and rejected his treaties as invalid. In 1824, MacCarthy and his hope for Africa were dead. The governor, who had interfered with their slave-trading operations, was killed by the Ashanti in a bloody skirmish near Nsamanko.

The British, whose colonial policies swung regularly between advance and retreat, considered withdrawing totally from West Africa after news of MacCarthy's death reached London. The uproar over the MacCarthy disaster died down, however, and a new governor, Charles Turner, was appointed. Turner shared MacCarthy's attitude toward slave trading. He, too, concluded treaties with the native rulers, particularly with the powerful Caulker family, which controlled territory near Freetown and on Sherbro Island off the coast. The British again disallowed each of these pacts because it correctly reasoned that Turner's government would be unable to administer these new regions.

Behind Freetown, in Sierra Leone's interior, tribal warfare had broken out between the Temne and Loko tribes. On the coast, the Caulkers, profiting from a clandestine slave trade, fought among themselves. These new developments were an ill omen for Sierra Leone, which had begun to progress through the export of timber, groundnuts, and palm oil. The oil from the groundnut, used in cooking, was in great demand in Europe. Palm oil, as has been said, was used as a lubricant and in soap, a necessity during the Industrial Revolution, which was now in full bloom. As the groundnut trade grew in importance, it was obvious that Sierra Leone had to gain greater control over the groundnut sources lest it attract other imperialists. But, in the 1840s, the British had no intention of committing themselves much further in West Africa despite the economic possibilities that lay in groundnut cultivation and the expanding palm oil trade. In Africa, Great Britain's colonial advance had momentarily stalled.

Politically, advances were being made by the black settlers. In 1845, William Fergusson, a West Indian, was appointed the colony's first black governor. Despite Fergusson's occupation of the governor's chair, the Sierra Leone government was still predominantly European.

In Fergusson's time, and during the two succeeding decades, groundnut and palm oil resources were exploited more fully and the British steamships that visited Freetown after 1852 speeded trade and caused a step-up in efforts to expand into the interior. Unfortunately, along the Melakori River, rich in groundnuts, the native planters were using slave labor supplied by the Caulkers and, when Creole traders moved into the region, they were expelled. The acting governor, Robert Dougan, dispatched an armed expedition to the area in 1855. Soon after their gunboat landed, they waded ashore and began to set fire to the settlement. The native planters took them by surprise and seventy-seven in the landing party were killed. Three years later, the government retaliated and the Melakori revolt was crushed. No provision had been made, however, to secure the area for Great Britain. Instead, the slave source of Sherbro Island was annexed in 1861, the same year Lagos was made part of Great Britain's West African empire.

In Freetown, the demands for black representation first articulated by the Nova Scotians in 1792 had never ceased. French activity to the north of the colony made it imperative that a working peace be achieved between the dissident groups in Freetown. In 1863, a move in this direction was made when executive and legislative councils were created. John Ezzidio, a former slave, became the first African to serve in the legislative body.

In the 1860s, the British found their West African

interests challenged, not only by the Ashanti nation, but by the rival French empire-builders. Few in Parliament had a keen desire to expand, for West Africa caused too many problems. Withdrawal proposals were heard again in the House of Commons. In an economy move, in 1865, it was decided to unite Great Britain's West African possessions. Gambia, the Gold Coast, Lagos, and Sierra Leone were to be ruled from Freetown. The avowed British policy was henceforth to be one of consolidation but, after 1865, the opposite was in fact the case. In reaction to French incursions, the British began to accumulate more territory.

In 1874, following the Ashanti war, the unwieldy union of Britain's West African colonies was dissolved. The British government would now insist that each of the colonies pay its own way through trade and customs duties.

The 1870s and 1880s were marked in Sierra Leone by an increase in domestic violence. Among the Caulkers, a leadership struggle was underway. When this issue was at last resolved, access to the oil palms became a bone of contention between the Creoles and the government. The European depression of the 1870s had caused a drop in the price of palm oil and Creole profits had declined sharply. The Creoles misread the situation. They claimed warring traders and unfriendly tribesmen were disrupting the palm oil trade and demanded that the government annex the oil palm regions to restore order. This, of course, was no solution, for it was the diminishing European demand that kept palm oil prices depressed.

The greatest threat to Sierra Leone and Great Britain in West Africa was yet to come. The French had expedited their treaty-making with the tribes of Guinea, north of Sierra Leone. In 1882, the French reached an accord with the Melakori chiefs, who occupied the territory where the 1855 debacle had taken place. The groundnut sources were now within the French orbit. In 1883, the Senegal valley was occupied. There was now a very real possibility that the French might move into the nearby Temne country despite diplomatic efforts by Sierra Leone's governor to forestall them.

The government in Sierra Leone now undertook a haphazard policy of concluding pacts with as many chiefs as possible. Clearly, however, this was a stop-gap procedure and an accommodation with the French had to be made before a head-on collision occurred. At Berlin, in 1884–1885, great progress was made along these lines and by 1895 the two imperial powers came to an agreement which gave Sierra Leone its final boundary with what became French Guinea. But, as in Berlin a decade earlier, the carving up of Sierra Leone's interior was arbitrary. The tribesmen were never consulted and chiefdoms were divided, part of them lying in French Guinea, part in Sierra Leone.

In 1896, claiming their decision was "in the best interests of the people," the British declared a protectorate over their share of Sierra Leone's interior.

The area was then divided into five districts, each ruled by a district commissioner appointed in Freetown. The more important native rulers were graced with the title of paramount chief, yet each district commissioner sat in judgment on major cases arising in each district. While the Paramount Chiefs had the appearance of power in their chiefdoms, the real and ultimate power rested with the district commissioner, the agent of the British colonial regime in Freetown. After 1896, Sierra Leone was composed of the 260-square-mile peninsula, which included Freetown and Sherbro Island and the newly acquired Protectorate. In comparison to the colony, the Protectorate was enormous — 27,000 square miles which contained a population many times greater than that of the coast.

Needless to say, there was much anger and frustration among the Protectorate tribes. This frustration boiled over in early 1898 when the Sierra Leone governor imposed a hut tax, which the chiefs feared would cost them their land. The actual revolt was sparked when one chief refused to pay his hut tax and a detachment of the hated Frontier Police came to arrest him. The conflict that ensued cost over one thousand lives. The Creoles suffered at the hands of the tribes, despite their opposition to many government policies, because of their privileged political and social status. The revolt was suppressed when the rebelling chief was caught and exiled. In a crude show of force following their victory, the Sierra Leone government marched one thousand soldiers through

the Protectorate as a warning to the defeated tribesmen against future uprisings. Despite resistance
by most tribesmen, the hut tax was retained.

For the next twenty years, Sierra Leone remained
relatively peaceful despite agitation by the Creoles
over the issue of representation on the law-making
legislative council. In 1920, delegates from all of
colonial West Africa met in Accra on the Gold
Coast. This group, known as the National Congress
of British West Africa, contained men whose loyalty
to the allied cause had been proven by their bravery
during the war. They now had organized to collect
their due — representation and a voice in determin-
ing the future of their homelands. This original
movement for political rights finally had effect. In
1924 Sierra Leone was given a new constitution,
general elections were held, and the legislative
council was enlarged. While the native population
benefited little because of property and literacy
requirements, Creole representation was increased.
In 1943, further reform brought more native Africans into the legislative council. Still, the native
Africans were subordinated to the Creoles, who
constituted less than three per cent of Sierra Leone's
population.

The discovery of iron and diamonds in the 1930s
and the improvement of roads, rail lines, and har-
bors placed Sierra Leone on firmer if not yet stable
ground economically when World War II ended in
1945. The election of a Labour government in England, committed to decolonization and self-rule,

promised major changes, not only for Sierra Leone but for the entire British Empire.

In 1947, a new constitution gave the Africans a majority on both the executive and legislative councils. The Creoles, numbering 60,000, bitterly opposed this democratic provision which would, in effect, shift the locus of power to the Protectorate's 2 million indigenous Africans. So adamant were the Creoles in their opposition that the constitution could not be implemented until 1951.

The man most responsible for the introduction of the new constitution was Dr. Milton Margai. Born in 1895, the son of a trader, Margai received his education in England. He became the first African from the Protectorate to receive a medical degree. Coincidentally, his brother Albert was the first Protectorate African to become a barrister. The Margai brothers were not Creoles and hence appealed to the people of the Protectorate, while their economic status made them acceptable to many Creoles. In 1950, Milton Margai founded the Sierra Leone People's Party which included Creoles as window dressing, but the SLPP was clearly a Protectorate party. Margai was, in fact, the leader of the anti-Creole forces. Pressure applied by the Sierra Leone People's Party resulted, in 1951, in enforcing the new constitution. Party rule was ushered in during the 1951 elections in which Margai's SLPP scored a resounding victory. Margai appointed only SLPP members to the executive council, a major step toward cabinet or party government. The government was now theoretically responsible to the electorate. Two years later, the party members on the executive council were given the rank of minister. In 1954, Dr. Margai was elevated to the post of chief minister. In 1956, the legislative council was replaced by a House of Representatives. The first election in which the people of the Protectorate (now called the Provinces) voted directly took place in 1957 and the SLPP won again. Dr. Milton Margai became Prime Minister in 1958. In 1959, he was knighted by Queen Elizabeth.

However, there was dissension within the ranks of the SLPP. Albert Margai differed with his brother over policy matters. With Siaka Stevens, he formed the People's National Party (PNP) in 1958 to attract those disillusioned with the SLPP and Milton Margai's leadership. This alliance was soon broken when the controversial and politically astute Stevens temporarily joined Sir Milton Margai in the short-lived United National Front. The UNF was organized in 1960 in preparation for constitutional talks which resulted in Sierra Leone's being granted independence from Great Britain on April 27, 1961. Stevens soon left the UNF and, with radical nationalist Wallace Johnson, created the All People's Congress (APC). The APC had the support of many young radicals and labor unionists. They succeeded in winning seats in the Freetown Municipal Elections, but their leaders, who presented a serious challenge to the Margai forces, were jailed for "traitorous acts." The charges were proven false and they were later acquitted. It was on this ominous note that Sierra Leone's independence began.

The elections of May 1962 were notable because, for the first time, the SLPP failed to win a majority. It was only when twelve independents allied themselves with Sir Milton's party that he was able to form a government. The next two years were difficult ones for the SLPP, made more so when Sir Milton Margai died suddenly in April 1964. His brother Albert, with whom he had been reconciled, was immediately called upon to form a new government. With Albert Margai as Prime Minister, the political alignments changed little as opposition to his government grew. Corruption from within became an overriding campaign issue and in the elections of March 1967, Siaka Stevens' party, the APC, garnered enough votes to win the general election. Unfortunately, Albert Margai was unwilling to relinquish the reins of power. A political vacuum was created, which the army quickly filled. For a year, the newly constituted National Reformation Council under Brigadier A. T. Juxon-Smith ruled Sierra Leone. In April 1968, a group of army warrant officers, in revolt over a pay dispute, toppled Juxon-Smith's NRC government. An interim committee was organized and, on April 26, 1968, Siaka Stevens, after a year's wait, became Prime Minister of Sierra Leone. While the return to civilian rule was a hopeful sign. the major problems—corruption and unemployment—which had pushed Sierra Leone to the verge of bankruptcy, were still there. As the year ended, outbreaks of violence in the provinces persuaded Prime Minister Stevens to declare a state of emergency.

The decree proved of little effect, however. Two attempts upon Stevens' life prompted the prime minister in April 1971 to demand from an obedient parliament sweeping, and unprecedented, powers to restore order to this troubled nation. With his popularity decreasing rapidly, Stevens has even imported troops from neighboring Guinea to act as his personal guard. Unfortunately, at this writing, Sierra Leone appears to be headed toward that unhappy situation which has frequently plagued many of Africa's young nations — one-man rule.

LIBERIA

"The Love of Liberty Brought us Here" — Liberian motto

IN 1790, 60,000 FREE NEGROES lived in the United States, a number that quadrupled by 1820. The majority of free blacks, as in England, were unskilled and impoverished, restricted by racist laws which closed many avenues of progress that might otherwise have been open to them. As the Negro population increased, so too did the white man's fear of his black brother. For the black in America, slave or free, the future was dim.

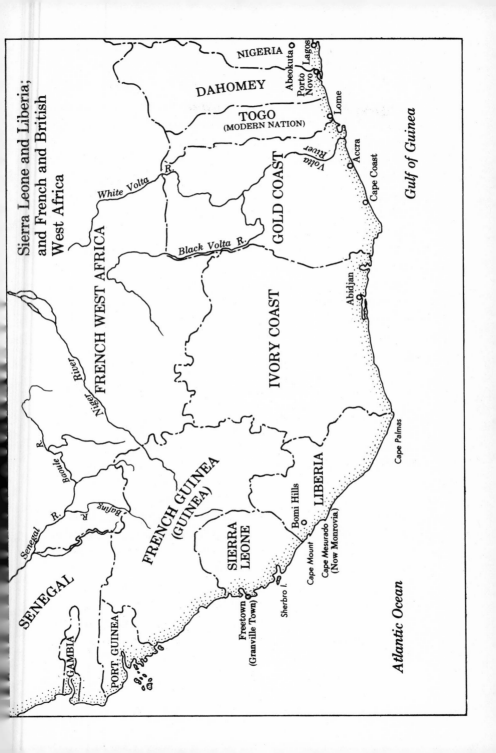

Sierra Leone and Liberia; and French and British West Africa

Thomas Jefferson was among the first to suggest that the free Negro be relocated on the vast, barely charted American continent. Jefferson thought of the Pacific Northwest; others considered Louisiana or a black state along the Missouri River. For thirty years various proposals were tossed about. In 1816, however, a group of men met in Washington with the intention of following through on the idea of black colonization. The result of this meeting was the formation of the American Society for Colonizing the Free People of Color in the United States, or, more simply, the American Colonization Society. Among the early sponsors of the ACS were such public figures as Henry Clay, Chief Justice John Marshall, Andrew Jackson, Francis Scott Key, Bushrod Washington (George Washington's nephew), and Senator John Randolph. The American Congress, in fact, was enthusiastic enough to vote the Society $100,000 with which to launch itself.

While many of the Society's supporters were motivated by humanitarian feelings, the concept of colonization had its seamier political overtones. The free black was a "problem" in the eyes of white America, and white attitudes and laws aggravated the "problem." There were Americans who realized that the motives of the Society may not have been as pure as they seemed. William Lloyd Garrison, the fiery orator and abolitionist, saw in the Society a vehicle for avoiding the social, economic, and political issues created by the peculiar American institution of slavery:

> I am prepared to show, that those who have entered into this conspiracy against human rights are unanimous in abusing their victims; . . . unanimous in proclaiming the absurdity, that our free blacks are natives of Africa; unanimous in propagating the libel, that they cannot be elevated and improved in this country; . . . unanimous in conceding the right of the planters to hold their slaves in a limited bondage; unanimous in their hollow pretence for colonizing, namely to evangelize Africa; unanimous in their *true motive* for the measure—a terror lest the blacks should rise to avenge their accumulated wrongs.[51]

There was more than a grain of truth in Garrison's indictment of the ACS. Many of its backers owned slaves, and free blacks in the midst of a slave-holding society caused the slaveholder great concern. Garrison contended that the idea of colonization "is a conspiracy to send the free people of color to Africa under a benevolent pretence, but really that the slaves may be held more securely in bondage. It is a conspiracy based upon fear, oppression, and falsehood, which draws its [strength] from the prejudices of the people," and added that:

> . . . our colored population are not aliens; they were born on our soil . . . their fathers fought bravely to achieve our independence during the revolutionary war, without immediate or subsequent compensation; they spilt their blood freely during the last war [1812]; they are entitled, in fact, to every inch of our southern and much of our western territory, having worn themselves out in its cultivation, and received nothing but wounds and bruises in return. Are these the men to stigmatize as foreigners?[52]

This speech was published in 1831 in Garrison's abolitionist newspaper, *The Liberator*, but its content is consistent with his position toward the ACS from the very date of its creation fifteen years earlier. Like the words of most prophets who oppose the tide of popular sentiment, Garrison's protests were virtually ignored, his voice drowned in the accolades for the colonization scheme. With Congressional money backing the venture, two agents were dispatched to Sierra Leone in November 1817, to investigate the possibility of establishing a colony there. The reception they received from the British government in Freetown was not particularly encouraging. Considering Sierra Leone's own difficulties, the British attitude was not surprising. However, an agreement was reached to permit a settlement on Sherbro Island, southeast of Freetown. The first volunteers, eighty-eight in all, arrived in 1820, the vanguard of an uneven stream of emigrants who would find their way back to their ancestral homeland during the nineteenth century.

While many of America's free blacks rejected the Society's repatriation efforts, there were others, such as Paul Cuffe, who saw in colonization a very real opportunity for the free black to improve himself. Born into poverty of Indian and Negro parents, Cuffe educated himself and became a wealthy merchant and shipowner. His own almost insurmountable problems confirmed his belief that, despite his own case, advancement for the black man in the United States was virtually impossible. With the assistance of the British-based African Association and the ACS, Cuffe traveled to Sierra Leone and succeeded, over the years, in encouraging quite a few free blacks to emigrate.

By 1820, the limited funds of the ACS were exhausted. But support for colonization had still another champion, President James Monroe. Another shipload of blacks was sent to Sierra Leone, this time under the banner of the United States government. As it turned out, the original Sherbro Island colony, conceived in hope, ended in disaster. By 1822, a combination of factors caused the settlement's demise. Among them were the climate, malaria, and consistent harrassment by local tribes over land rights. The survivors of the doomed experiment returned to the Sierra Leone mainland. Agents were again commissioned to secure territory for a colony. The coast was scoured for a suitable location by Matthew Perry, the American officer who "opened" Japan to the West two decades later, and Providence Island in the Cape Mesurado lagoon was chosen. The only drawback was the local ruler, King Peter, who had no interest in disposing of his property. The agents, untrained in the finer arts of diplomacy, held a gun to the king's head until he agreed to sell his land for about $300 in guns, tobacco, and beads.

In July 1822, fifty black settlers, under the command of a white visionary named Jehudi Ashmun, debarked at Cape Mesurado, the strip of land which would eventually be rechristened Monrovia in hon-

or of the ACS's benefactor, James Monroe. Within
four years, Ashmun had established himself as head
of the new colony. Almost immediately, he moved
to suppress the slave trade which plagued Sierra
Leone also and which Ashmun knew would have to
be eradicated, if Liberia were to grow and prosper.
Despite the fact that, in 1819, the death penalty had
been ordered by the United States government for
slave trading, the traffic still flourished along the
West African coast. Enforcement of the anti-slave
trade laws was difficult, and the demand for slaves
made slaving worth the risk. Ashmun, however, took
the lead and conducted raids against the local slave
dealers. With the help of American cruisers, the
slave trade — at least in the immediate area of Cape
Mesurado — was greatly reduced.

In the United States, the colonization movement
gained adherents as slave rebellions increased. In
particular, when Nat Turner led his band of slaves
on a murderous rampage in 1831, the ACS coffers
subsequently swelled.

New colonization efforts, independent of the
ACS and threatening its authority over the 130-mile
stretch of coastline, were attempted. In 1833, the
first of these unrelated organizations to undertake a
separate settlement was the Maryland Colonization
Society which chose to locate in the Cape Palmas
region. Another such group, the Mississippi Colonization Society, chartered in 1836, failed and was
eventually absorbed into the ACS. The most tragic
of these colonization debacles was that begun by a

group of Quakers in 1834. Shortly after landing they were attacked by neighboring tribes who viewed the colonists as intruders. Deeply committed to the principles of non-violence, the Quakers were soon massacred.

By 1839, with the exception of the land controlled by the Maryland Colonization Society, the various settlements were united and the Commonwealth of Liberia was born. Its first governor was Thomas Buchanan, a cousin of President James Buchanan.

Liberia's legal position, however, remained unclear. Although it was supported by American money, it was not a colony of the United States. Its government and settlers were in perpetual conflict with local tribes over titles to land. The settlers barely exceeded two thousand. The Commonwealth of Liberia was, in fact, a stepchild, an oddity, for which no nation was willing to assume responsibility.

When Great Britain queried the United States as to whether Liberia was under its protection, the United States gave a vague reply. At home, interest in colonization had declined and the ACS, barely able to support itself, declared Liberia an independent entity in 1846. On July 27, 1847, Liberia became a republic. Its constitution was almost identical to that of the United States. In 1848, Great Britain extended diplomatic recognition to the new republic. France followed suit in 1852. The United States, however, held back, its hesitation caused by the power of pro-slavery interests in Washington

who were thoroughly opposed to recognizing a
black nation. In the tense political atmosphere that
marked pre-Civil War America, there was little
open support for the recognition of either Liberia or
the black Caribbean republic of Haiti. Finally, on
December 3, 1861, with the Civil War in its early
stages, President Abraham Lincoln declared that "if
any good reason exists why we should persevere
longer in withholding our recognition of the independence and sovereignty of Hayti and Liberia, I am
unable to discern it." In June 1862, the Republic of
Liberia was recognized by the United States Congress. The African stepchild had become a full-
fledged nation.

Liberia's first president was Joseph Jenkins Roberts, a Virginia-born octoroon. Roberts, who arrived
in Liberia in 1829, had served as the Commonwealth's first governor of black descent, from 1841
until it became a republic six years later, and then as
its president until 1856. Like the United States,
the Liberian government's functions were divided
amont an executive branch, a congress, and a supreme
court. With independence came the emergence of
a political party, the True Liberian or Republican
party, founded by President Roberts. The True
Liberian party remained in power until 1869, when
its hold over Liberian politics was broken as new
political coalitions arose. By the 1850s Liberia's
trade had begun to expand as more merchant ships
from both Europe and America arrived at Monrovia.
One of these was the *Termagant,* commanded by

Theodore Canot, a reformed slave trader who extolled the virtues of the new Liberian republic:

> I had no difficulty in finding all sorts of workmen in Monrovia, for the colonists brought with them all the mechanical ingenuity and thrift which characterize the American people. . . . Had nature bestowed a better harbor on the Mesurado river, and afforded a safer entrance for large vessels, Monrovia would now be second only to Sierra Leone. . . . The amplest proof has been given of the soil's fertility in the production of coffee, sugar, cotton and rice. I have frequently seen a cane fourteen feet high, and as thick as any I ever met with in the [West] Indies. Throughout the entire jurisdiction between Cape Mount and Cape Palmas [the farthest western and eastern points], . . . the soil is equally prolific.[53]

Canot's enthusiasm was admirable though it was exaggerated. Liberia was still hampered by incredible poverty; the vast majority of the people shared little in the slim profits from their nation's resources.

In 1857, the Maryland Colonization Society, Maryland in Africa, brought her territory into the republic. Although Monrovia claimed much of the territory of what was and is still called the Hinterland — the inland area behind the coast — it did in fact control only the coast. As the imperial appetites of England and France grew, Liberia's extravagant territorial claims were called into question. She was unable to defend them or show that she had effectively occupied these areas.

Added to her external problems was the political and racial conflict within Liberia. Aside from the bloody battles with the Grebo, Mandingo, and Kru—the tribes from whom the original settlers had first usurped land—there was trouble among the settlers themselves. There were only 3,000 colonists in 1850, but the population began to swell as "recaptives" were landed in Liberia as well as Sierra Leone. These "Congoes," as they were known in both Sierra Leone and Liberia, became a formidable political force. In the 1856 presidential election, Joseph Jenkins Roberts was rejected in favor of his darker-skinned opponent, Stephen Benson. Race was fast becoming a qualification for holding office in Liberia. This racial-political alignment intensified with the election of Ohio-born Edward Roye, in 1870. Roye was the first "full-blooded" black president of Liberia. Race proved no qualification for office, however, for Roye's regime ended in chaos and economic disaster for which he was primarily responsible. In 1872, he was deposed and jailed. The end of the unhappy affair came when Roye escaped from jail and tried to get away in a canoe. It capsized and the disgraced ex-president drowned.

The Liberian counterpart of the Creoles of Sierra Leone were the Americo-Liberians, descendants of the original settlers. The Americo-Liberians created their own political machine, the True Whig party, which came to power in 1877. Since then, the True Whigs have never relinquished their control over Liberian politics.

As Liberia's politics suffered the ups and downs usual in any new nation attempting to stabilize it-

self, so did its economy. In the last quarter of the
nineteenth century, coffee, rubber, cocoa, and palm
oil were exported in greater quantities than they
had been in Canot's day. The United States, England, Holland, and Germany were Liberia's main
markets. Yet, despite the improvement in trade, the
economy was in dire straits, the encroaching imperialist powers placed Liberia's sovereignty in danger,
and Liberia's twenty indigenous tribes—particularly
the seafaring Kru—were openly hostile to the Liberian government. France, advancing from the north
and east, offered Liberia protectorate status. The
English proposed an Anglo-American protectorate.
The United States, not yet an active member of the
imperialist club, protested, and both European nations backed off, content to nibble away at Liberia's
borders. Finally, in 1911-12, a boundary treaty was
signed. Its terms required Liberia to relinquish to
the British in Sierra Leone and the French in Guinea and the Ivory Coast nearly one third of the disputed Hinterland.

The twentieth century opened as the nineteenth
century had ended for Liberia. She remained a bank-
rupt and clumsy oligarchic dictatorship balanced
precariously on an almost American-style plantation
system, replete with antebellum-style mansions—a
society that mocked the principles on which the nation was conceived. The True Whig party, the tool
of the Americo-Liberian clique, governed Liberia by
force for the benefit of the wealthy. Domestic economic and political reforms, which might have put

Liberia on a steadier keel and improved her relations with the colonial powers, were ignored. Loans were floated and never repaid, threats and ultimatums were issued by Liberia's foreign creditors. Liberia answered these demands with promises that were rarely fulfilled and only an occasional visit by American warships in the pre-World War I era of "gunboat diplomacy" prevented a European takeover. The deterioration of Liberia continued until Germany, France, Great Britain, and the United States decided to organize a consortium, which had as its sole purpose the collecting of loans made and then defaulted upon by Liberia. Only the outbreak of war, in which the member nations were on opposing sides, stopped the consortium from carrying out its intentions.

In 1914, the Americo-Liberian government was being challenged from within by the Kru peoples and by other heavily taxed and oppressed Liberian tribes. Intervention by the United States, which had not yet entered World War I, saved Liberia from a popular revolution. Anti-government outbreaks continued into the 1930s as the entrenched Americo-Liberians permitted the exploitation and abuse of the native tribes to continue unchecked. As late as 1922, American President Warren Harding resurrected the protectorate scheme. But the era of isolation was already upon America. The chances of the United States declaring a protectorate over Liberia were less than remote, considering that she had refused to join the League of Nations, an organization that had President Woodrow Wilson as its guiding light. The United States Senate, true to isolationist form, rejected Harding's proposal.

Liberia remained an area whose resources had not been fully developed. The American Firestone Company, in 1925, was the first major American corporation to take advantage of Liberia's potential. It acquired a one-hundred-year lease to one million acres and began to cultivate rubber plants to fill the demand for rubber products, especially automobile tires, in the United States. Rubber, in fact, accounted for ninety per cent of Liberia's exports before 1950. In return for the use of Liberia's fertile land, Firestone extended to the Liberian government a loan of $5 millions. A punishing service charge was applied to the loan, amounting to almost half the Liberian government's total revenue for 1931. Considering Liberia's frail economic position, this arrangement was of the greatest benefit to the American Firestone Company. The contract, negotiated during the term of Liberian president Charles D. B. King, remained a source of friction between subsequent Liberian governments and Firestone.

More shocking than this blatant example of economic exploitation were the ugly rumors that domestic slavery and forced labor were being used on the rubber plantations. Thomas J. R. Faulkner, a presidential candidate who lost to Charles D. B. King, made a tour of the United States in 1927. While there he charged that slavery and similar abuses of human rights were prevalent in Liberia. In

1929, the U.S. State Department succeeded in forcing Liberia to accept an investigation by the League of Nations. This commission's report supported many of Faulkner's allegations. It found that contract labor was being exported to the cocoa plantations of Fernando Po, a Spanish colony off the West African coast. Forced labor was found to be common within Liberia, and Liberians themselves, subject to fines of one sort or another, would "pawn" relatives into contract slavery in order to pay the fines. This scandal rocked the Liberian government from top to bottom. President King and Vice-President Allen Yancy were implicated. King was forced to resign and Yancy was impeached. Edwin Barclay, a political power in his own right, replaced Charles King as president.

Under Edwin Barclay the first meaningful reforms took place. He shepherded Liberia through the depression-ridden 1930s and, during his administration, the abuses of King's regime were, for the most part, eliminated.

In 1943, Edwin Barclay decided to step down. His hand-picked presidential successor was William Vacanarat Shadrach Tubman. Born in 1895, the son of a Methodist minister, Tubman had served in the Liberian Senate during the King years. As he progressed up the political ladder, Tubman aligned himself with Barclay's forces. William Tubman's avowed commitment when he became president was to integrate the indigenous tribesmen — the Kru, Kpelle, Bassa, Grebo, Vai, Mandingo, Gio and Gola — and the America-Liberians into a cohesive society. This was to be Tubman's reunification policy. Suffrage was extended to hut owners and tribal Africans, who compose a majority of the Liberian population. They were also appointed to positions of prestige and importance such as the Supreme Court and the Presidential Cabinet. The fraudulent acquisition of land from indigenous tribesmen by America-Liberians was halted. While the results of these policies have not been entirely satisfactory, there has indeed been a political as well as psychological Africanization in the Liberia of William Tubman.

On the economic front, Tubman pushed for reform. The Firestone Company was forced to release eighty per cent of its acreage and new taxes were levied on its exports. In 1953, an income tax of twenty-five per cent was imposed on Firestone's Liberian profits. Realizing that the Liberian economy was based on one crop — rubber — Tubman sought to attract foreign investment through an "open door" policy.

Over forty foreign companies accepted the Liberian invitation. Many of these corporations were involved in developing the mining operations centered in the Bomi Hills north of Monrovia. Iron ore, in the 1950s, exceeded rubber as Liberia's major export. Unfortunately, the people of Liberia did not profit in proportion to their nation's economic growth. John Gunther, who visited Liberia in 1955, observed that "Liberia is roughly the size of Ohio . . . but the entire country has only ten miles of

paved road, five of which are in the capital. . . . Today Liberia produces enough rubber for thousands
of American cars to ride on, but two-thirds of the
country cannot be reached except on foot."[54] Gunther also noted that more than ninety per cent of Liberia's population was illiterate, corruption existed
on all government levels, and the average wage was
less than one dollar a day.

While political representation was expanded,
President Tubman began to arrogate more power to
his own office. In 1951, the constitution was amend-
ed to enable Tubman to serve an unlimited number
of terms. In 1955, he was re-elected easily. Following the election, the rival Reformation and Independent True Whig Parties were outlawed. In the
1959 "contest" Tubman received 530,000 votes, his
opponent 59. Dihdwo Twe, the candidate of Kru
dissidents, who had the courage to oppose Tubman,
had to flee Liberia. Opposition to William Tubman
was now equated with treason. The legislature,
whose demise began under Edwin Barclay, became
President Tubman's rubber stamp.

While Tubman could control and direct the affairs
of Liberia with little fear of contradiction or effective opposition, the more militant nations of Africa
have caused him some concern. Nationalism is
contagious and, despite Tubman's reunification
schemes, it could easily take hold in Liberia, where
the native tribesmen far outnumber the elite
Americo-Liberians. In order to deflect or forestall
this development, Tubman hosted the 1961 Mon-

rovia Conference of newly independent nations. Although nationalist hostility, within and beyond Liberia's borders, has been temporarily neutralized, it has not been effaced. Liberia is still regarded by many African leaders as an outpost of white imperialism on West Africa's coast.

However, during the 1960s there were encouraging signs. The literacy levels were raised; the public health service, which was only begun in 1931, has improved steadily; and the budget in 1968 soared to $68 millions, as compared with $1 million in 1945. Despite the considerable economic advances that have taken place in the last decade, with the injection of technical and financial aid from other countries and international organizations, the Republic of Liberia is still an impoverished nation.

William Tubman announced in 1968, at the outset of his sixth term as president, that it would be his last. He even permitted criticism of his regime during the showcase trial of a Liberian diplomat charged with subversive activities. Yet, though the iron hand of William Tubman's rule has been lifted slightly, Liberia remains a question mark in the 1970s.

(As we go to press, word has arrived of President Tubman's death, in London, on July 23, 1971.)

CHAPTER FIVE

Exploration and Partition: the Scramble for Africa

The Signatory Powers of the present (Berlin) Act recognize the obligation to insure the establishment of authority in regions occupied by them on the coasts of the African continent sufficient to protect existing rights, and . . . freedom of trade and of transit under the conditions agreed upon. — Article XXXV, *The Berlin Act*, 1885[55]

Africa was a melon, and it was duly portioned out. — JOHN GUNTHER, 1955.[56]

THE LAST TWO DECADES of the nineteenth century are usually referred to as the time of the "Scramble," the period when Europe's powers competed against one another for African territory. It was during these years that the imperial quest intensified. Centuries of exploitation of Africa's resources, particularly the millions of her peoples enslaved and transported from their native land, had brought riches to many a European merchant. Africa's other products—gold, palm kernels, pepper, groundnuts, and ivory—were also prized. In retrospect, however, it appears that the profits made in legitimate trade with Africa were minuscule when compared with the fortunes that were made from

144

shipping European manufactures to the Americas or east of Suez. New markets for Europe's goods were a factor in sparking the Scramble, but its causes were far more complex than the search for new markets and raw materials.

After the rise of a unified Germany in the 1860s and 1870s under Otto von Bismarck's leadership, strategic and political considerations kept Europe in turmoil. Alliances between powers were proposed and scrapped as each European nation grew more distrustful of the others. The national rivalries the Europeans initially played out on their own soil were destined to be exported to Africa. Unfortunately, Africa would serve as a pawn, partitioned by the imperialists to settle home-grown European disputes.

A century before Africa's final partition, Europeans were developing an insatiable appetite for information about Africa and her peoples. In the late eighteenth and early nineteenth century, a time noted by its "hunger for discovery," interest in Africa's unknown hinterland increased enormously. Europe's sea-going nations and the United States had been long familiar with West Africa's coast when for hundreds of years they had settled and plied their trade. But the strange, forbidding interior remained a mystery, an enigma which could be solved only by venturing inland.

In 1788, a group of wealthy Englishmen banded together and organized the Association for the Discovery of the Interior Parts of Africa, the pioneering circle of adventurers which came to be known as the African Association. Its declared purpose was to explore and thereby open Africa to the eyes of the world and thus promote legitimate trade with her peoples. About this time, too, the abolitionist movements in England and France were beginning to attract adherents. The anti-slavery men hoped that the African Association would spearhead the drive to replace the slave traffic with legitimate commerce, an exchange from which both European and African could benefit. Naturally, the African Association enjoyed the wholehearted support of the abolitionists.

The African Association concentrated its early efforts in exploring the Niger River where much of West Africa's trade, legitimate and otherwise, was centered. By 1795, four explorers had been sent forth under the Association's auspices. All failed to trace the mighty river's course, three of them dying in transit. The fifth to accept the Association's sponsorship was a young Scot, Mungo Park, who was commissioned to gather data on "the rise, the course and the termination of the Niger and of the various Nations which inhabit its borders." It was believed such direct contact could be useful in developing legitimate trade and perhaps also in persuading the peoples of the region to abandon the trade in slaves, which still flourished unchecked. Park, however, encountered hostility from Muslim traders as well as African tribesmen. His stores were pilfered, his companions fell ill, and more than once Park had to flee for his life. Yet he partly accomplished what he had set out to do. He proved, contrary to contemporary European belief, that the Niger flowed eastward. Park recorded the important discovery with his customary eloquence:

> As I was anxiously looking around for the river, one of them [his guides] called out, *geo affilli*, [see the water]; and looking forwards, I saw with infinite pleasure the great object of my mission; the long sought for, majestic Niger, glittering to the morning sun, as broad as the Thames at Westminster, and flowing slowly to the *eastward*. I hastened to the brink, and, having drank of the water, lifted up my fervent thanks in prayer, to the Great Ruler of all things for having thus far crowned my endeavours with success.[57]

While the direction of the Niger had been ascertained, its full course, from its source to its mouth, had yet to be sailed by a European. It was partly for this purpose that Park returned to West Africa in 1805. The Scot's second expedition, however, ended in tragedy. Halfway down the Niger at Bussa, Park and his disease-ravaged crew were attacked by enraged tribesmen. During the skirmish, Park's canoe capsized and he drowned.

Park's sad demise did not dampen the Association's enthusiasm. Other expeditions were mounted, but none scored a telling success until 1822 when an Englishman, Hugh Clapperton, departed from Tripoli and headed southward. Clapperton intended to cross the Sahara, establishing on his way a trade route to the Niger. Once there, he would then follow its course to the sea. Clapperton also planned to negotiate anti-slave trade treaties with the Muslim and African rulers he encountered during his travels. While he and his companions did "discover" Lake Chad and were welcomed into the Fulani courts of Kano and Sokoto, Clapperton came to the harsh realization that the heralded overland route was impractical. His journal provided much fascinating material on the Western and Central Sudan's Muslim civilization, but his main objective, the charting of the Niger, was not accomplished. In April 1826, Hugh Clapperton died at Sokoto on his second expedition.

Intrigued by the efforts of Park and Clapperton, an ambitious Frenchman named René Caillé left North Africa in 1827 and, often disguising himself as an Arab, made his way across the Sahara to the once-magnificent city of Timbuktu. The Muslim cultural center had by then become a minor trading post. With the rest of the Western Sudan, it had fallen on hard times, visible evidence that after the arrival of the Europeans the Western Sudan had stagnated as political power and trade had been drawn westward to the teeming trading towns of the Guinea coast. Caillé recrossed the Sahara, becoming the first European in modern times to survive and return from such a trip.

Accompanying Hugh Clapperton on his last, fateful adventure was another Englishman, Richard Lander. After Clapperton's death, Lander planned to return to England. Unwilling to retrace the expedition's trek across the Sahara, Lander decided to pursue the Niger to the sea. He was soon overtaken by a cavalry detachment from the Fulani-ruled Hausa kingdom of Zaria. Although he was detained, Lander was not harmed. He gained his release in 1828 and returned to England. In 1830, this time accompanied by his brother John, Lander returned to West Africa intent on sailing the full length of the Niger to its mouth. With a canoe as their means of transportation, the Landers paddled down the Niger from Bussa, the scene of Park's death, to Brass Town in the Niger Delta. From this depot, they boarded an English ship and in November 1830 passed into the Gulf of Guinea. Another misconception — that the Niger was a branch of the Congo — was now dispelled. At last, the Niger had been conquered, a third of a century after Mungo Park's exploits had captured the European imagination.

Richard Lander, like so many of the Niger's explorers, died violently. In 1834, while attached to shipbuilder Macgregor Laird's expedition, Lander was mortally wounded in a battle with African traders up in arms over the influx of Europeans into an area they considered their exclusive province. His brother John died in London five years later.

During the 1840s, failure mixed liberally with success as expedition followed expedition into Africa's interior. Humanitarians, businessmen, and missionaries published a mountain of memoirs recounting their first-hand experiences. Europe's interest in Africa was never permitted to flag after the explorers had drawn aside the curtain that once veiled Africa from European eyes.

It was the missionary, committed to converting

the African "savage" to Christianity and abolishing
the slave trade, who was probably most responsible
for the increased encroachment of Europe into Africa. The treaties entered into by European consuls
with strong religious bents, particularly Governor
Charles MacCarthy in Sierra Leone and John Beecroft in the Niger Delta, inevitably involved the
European in internal African affairs. While the home
government usually invalidated treaties and pacts
signed without their consent, the invisible line,
which formerly separated the European and African
spheres of influence — one limited to the coast, the
other to the interior — was repeatedly crossed and
clashes between each became more frequent. There
was no question that it was morally correct to suppress slaving and end the horror and suffering of its
victims. Yet European intervention, however humane
its motivation, smoothed the way for another evil —
imperialism.

By the 1850s, African exploration became commonplace. Each fresh venture into the unknown interior aroused new interest. With improved communications — steamers regularly visited West Africa
after 1852 — each expedition was publicized widely
in Europe, often at the expense of fact. Much of the
exploring activity had by this time shifted to Central and East Africa where John Speke and his col-
league, Richard Burton, came upon Lake Victoria in
1858. Six years later, Sir Samuel White and his wife
reached Lake Albert. Earlier in the decade, Heinrich
Barth, a German traveling under a British flag,

crossed the Sahara and discovered the Upper Benue River, the important Niger tributary. During his wanderings, Barth passed through the Fulani-controlled cities of Sokoto, Katsina, and Timbuktu. His reminiscences are still considered an invaluable wellspring of information about nineteenth-century Nigeria.

The most celebrated of the nineteenth-century explorers and the individuals who made Africa a topic of popular conversation throughout Europe and the Americas were Dr. David Livingstone and Henry M. Stanley. Livingstone, a medical missionary, began his African experience in South Africa. While traveling northeast, he became the first known European to view the breathtaking Victoria Falls in Rhodesia. His fame was already spread worldwide when it was reported that he had fallen ill. The New York *Herald*, sensing a news story that could well become the most sensational of the century, assigned a young Welsh-born journalist, Henry M. Stanley, to find Dr. David Livingstone.

Stanley departed from Zanzibar on the East African coast in 1871. In November his party reached Livingstone's encampment on Lake Tanganyika's eastern shore. When he finally saw the haggard, tired missionary, he uttered his famous greeting: "Dr. Livingstone, I presume?" The men spent four months together. When Stanley finally bid Livingstone goodbye, Livingstone was gravely ill. His condition deteriorated and, in May 1873, he died. The meeting with the renowned Livingstone vaulted the flamboyant reporter from total obscurity to a fame which even the self-aggrandizing Stanley could not have imagined.

The Livingstone manhunt attracted the attention of the Belgian royal adventurer, Leopold II. Leopold II, King of the Belgians, was an imperialist's imperialist, a man committed to turning fantasy into reality. With Stanley as his consort and alter ego, he unleashed the forces that transformed Africa from an unknown entity into a massive European province. In 1876, the International Association for the Exploration and Civilization of Central Africa was formed in Brussels under Leopold's aegis. Despite its impressive crusading title, the International Association's overriding interest was less the "civilizing" of Africans than the exploitation of the continent's mineral resources, particularly those of the Congo region. The Belgian king chose the ubiquitous Henry M. Stanley to lead his imperial expedition and bring his grandiose colonial scheme to fruition. This was in 1877. The Scramble, which would change the political face of Africa, was now officially underway. European imperialism would henceforth follow a more determined, aggressive, and frantic course.

To gain a perspective on the Scramble and follow its progress, it is necessary to review the colonial positions of each European power at its outset. In general, with the exception of South Africa and Algeria in North Africa, European influence was limited to the African coasts. In West Africa, few

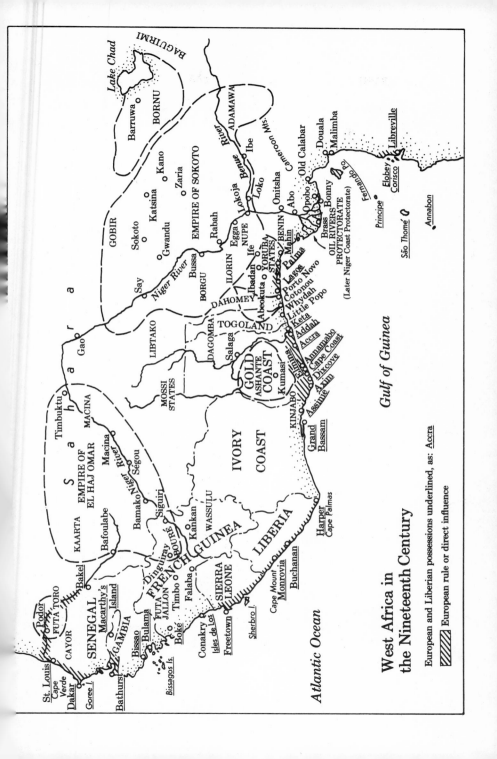

West Africa in
the Nineteenth Century

European and Liberian possessions underlined, as: <u>Accra</u>

///// European rule or direct influence

Europeans had penetrated more than a short distance into the hinterland. France had been stymied in her efforts to found plantations in Senegal's interior and was spending her time and efforts consolidating her possessions on the west coast. Particularly under the leadership of Louis Faidherbe, the French governor of Senegal (1854–1865), forts were maintained along the Guinea coast, at Whydah, Porto Novo, and Cotonou. Faidherbe was ever aware of the need to cultivate African rulers. He was markedly successful in developing a quasi-alliance with King Gelele of Dahomey.

In this pre-Scramble period, the French sought principally to encircle England's colonies of Gambia and Sierra Leone in order to abort any British move inland and also to corner the groundnut trade. After Faidherbe, French imperialism in Africa stalled when the armies of Napoleon III were overwhelmed and his empire crumbled in the Franco-Prussian War (1870–1871). But, by 1879, France was on the move once more. Cotonou, in Dahomey, had been ceded to her the year before and French traders had invaded the Niger Delta, long considered to be within Great Britain's unofficial domain. In addition, work was begun on a railway which would, on completion, stretch from Dakar in Senegal to Bamako on the Niger.

In 1881, Tunis in North Africa was occupied and two years later Porto Novo was formally placed under French protection. French influence over the Ivory Coast and Gabon, where the Italian-born

French officer, Savorgnan de Brazza, had signed treaties with the local rulers, increased sharply. It was now apparent to all that France was attempting to enclose North and Central Africa into an empire which would reach from Dakar on the Atlantic eastward across the Sahara to Djibouti in Somaliland on the Red Sea and southward from Algeria to the Congo.

On the eve of the Scramble, the British still adhered to a policy of official reticence. Their announced reluctance to pursue a forward policy was not borne out by their actions in West Africa or elsewhere. Again it must be mentioned that Great Britain's imperialism was more negative than positive in its execution. In other words, the British engaged in a defensive game of imperial chess, the ultimate aim of which was to checkmate the other powers, particularly France. West Africa was of little strategic value on an international scale, especially after the opening of the Suez Canal in 1869, which gave Great Britain a shortcut to her lucrative eastern possessions and markets. However, the "free trading" British feared that the French would impose tariffs on her West African traders. Great Britain's West African colonies were in generally poor economic condition. Sierra Leone and Gambia were impoverished; Lagos and the Gold Coast were becoming more costly to administer, but there was the promise of growing revenue from their trade.

During the nineteenth century, Parliamentary reports more than once suggested abandoning West

Africa but the outcries of Great Britain's merchants and later the appearance of the French killed these proposals. Despite her foothold in West Africa, colonialism for the British in the 1870s and 1880s did not seem a viable economic proposition. African clients proved unable to govern themselves, and the West African political and economic situation became more tense and fraught with danger. Great Britain found herself assuming a more active role in the internal affairs of West Africa, something she wished to avoid, if only for economic reasons.

When the French appeared in the Niger Delta, in Sierra Leone's hinterland, and along the banks of the Congo, posing a threat to British trade and traders in each area, the British government was forced to react lest the French annex the regions and make Great Britain's coveted principle of free trade a dead letter. To forestall this development, the British permitted the National African Company (chartered in 1886 as the Royal Niger Company) to act as its agent to acquire as much territory and exert as much influence as possible to block France's imperial design. With George Goldie at the helm, it managed to force or buy out French traders in the Niger. By the time the Berlin Conference opened in 1884 (see page 159), the lower reaches of the Niger were securely within what was later known as the Oil Rivers Protectorate.

Leopold and Stanley, meanwhile, had made incredible progress. The International Association's flag had been raised over much of what would be-

come the Congo Independent or Free State south of
the Congo River. The king's venture, in fact, was
among the major factors which conspired to hasten
the European partition of Africa.

Elsewhere in Africa, another event was taking
place which would add yet another element to the
confusion. In 1882, the British occupied Egypt following a revolt by the Egyptian army. The Suez
Canal was now under *de facto* British control. But
Great Britain realized that without the support of
the other European powers, she could not maintain
her grip on either Egypt or the Suez Canal.

Enter Otto von Bismarck, chancellor of Germany,
and Europe's acknowledged master of the diplomatic arts. There was no limit to the strategic and
political gains that Germany could realize if Bismarck played his African cards wisely. The French
burned with a desire for revenge since the loss of
Alsace-Lorraine in the Franco-Prussian War. Upper-
most in Bismarck's mind was the formulation of a
policy that would deflect French hostility in Europe
by encouraging her colonial desires in Africa. He
was aware that Germany's border with France would
be safe and secure only when France was relieved of
her obsession to recapture Alsace-Lorraine and
avenge her national honor.

Bismarck decided to support French claims to the
north bank of the Congo which were currently being disputed by Portugal. The British, who feared a
French takeover of the Congo's mouth, revived
an old treaty scheme which would recognize Portu-

guese rights to the region and in effect block
France's path both to the Atlantic and north from
the Congo to West and Central Africa. But Great
Britain's need for German support of her Egyptian
occupation proved the undoing of this proposal
when it became clear that the Germans were going
to side with the French. In 1884, the Anglo-Portu-
guese treaty was dropped.

Bismarck increased the pressure against the British in West Africa by declaring a protectorate in
April 1884 over what became German Southwest
Africa. He followed this act three months later with
another over Togoland and Kamerun (the Cameroons) after "treaties" with local chiefs were concluded by the German explorer, Gustav von Nachti-
gal. Nigeria was thus isolated, bordered on the
southeast by Kamerun and on the west by the
French in Dahomey.

King Leopold, who played so decisive a role in
setting the Scramble in motion, was busily securing
his own position. He agreed to a French demand
that, if he was unable to administer the Congo Free
State, it would revert to France. In return, France,
then Germany and the United States, recognized the
Congo Free State.

The speed with which annexations in Africa was
proceeding made it imperative that if a clash of
some magnitude were to be avoided, something had
to be done about regularizing the process of partition. With the French in his camp—at least as far as
Africa was concerned—Bismarck proposed that a

conference be held in Berlin to iron out the problems arising from the land grab. Fourteen nations
were invited to participate, including the United
States. Representatives from the remaining independent West African kingdoms and nations were
absent from this convocation, which set the ground
rules for the partition of their homeland. The Berlin
Conference for West Africa opened on November
15, 1884. The major items on the agenda were the
status of international trade and navigation on the
Congo and navigation of the Niger. Also, the circumstances under which a claim to a piece of West
African territory could be considered valid were to
be defined. No territorial questions were decided by
the conference itself. It was outside the sessions and
during the years following that Africa was carved up
by Europe's diplomats in meeting rooms thousands
of miles from the Niger and the Congo. Few of
these imperialists had ever set foot on African soil,
yet their decisions sealed the fate and governed the
future of millions.

When the Berlin Conference ended in February
1885, the signatories to the ensuing agreement recognized the Congo Free State and guaranteed freedom of commerce and navigation in the Congo's
basin and mouth. The navigation of the Niger was to
remain unencumbered, though Great Britain's
"sphere" over the river, thanks to Goldie, was implicitly recognized. For new annexations to be considered "legitimate," a European nation now had to
"effectively occupy" the region in question. The

term "effective occupation" was vague enough to permit each imperial nation its own interpretation and, rather than solving the problem of territorial claims, it confused the issue even more. As an after-thought, a few brief phrases expressing concern for the African's welfare and calling for the slave trade's suppression were added to the protocol. This was truly an accurate measure of the European power brokers' concern for the African peoples.

After 1885, French and British activity in West Africa mushroomed once more. The Ivory Coast was reoccupied in 1886 and Conakry, in what became French Guinea, was taken a year later. By 1891, the British colony of Sierra Leone was surrounded on three sides by the crescent-shaped French Guinea. In the West African interior, the French were faced with the equally imperial-minded African rulers, Ahmadu Séku, the son of El-Hajj Umar, and the persistent Samori Touré. El-Hajj Umar and Samori were overcome, along with the last independent Dahomean king, Behanzin, by 1894, though Samori lingered on, harassing his enemies until his capture in 1898.

The intensity of the imperial push of France and Great Britain made confrontation inevitable. In 1890, the European rivals met again to forestall such a happening. The resulting joint declaration sup-ported Great Britain's claims to the lower Niger. Most of the Fulani emirates under the Sultan of Sokoto's hegemony were assigned to Great Britain by the agreement. The French were acknowledged to hold sway from Say on the Niger eastward to Lake Chad. The Sultanate of Sokoto formed the frontier between the rival spheres.

The last decade of the nineteenth century saw the French unleash a three-pronged advance intended to make their trans-African empire a reality. From North Africa, Senegal, and the French Congo, French columns marched into the African hinterland.

The British, through George Goldie's Royal Niger Company, had even before Berlin been chipping away at Yorubaland. By 1888 most of Yorubaland had become part of the Lagos protectorate. In 1893, the former Oil Rivers Protectorate became the Niger Coast Protectorate as more of Nigeria's hinterland was incorporated into it. With Great Britain's official compliance, Goldie removed all stops. The Royal Niger Company's frenetic treaty-making during this last, most important decade of the nineteenth century, mirrored the equally hurried drive of the French.

Despite the 1890 agreement, the concord regarding frontiers and borders in West Africa was either misinterpreted (the western boundary of Nigeria had not been fixed) or was unacceptable to the French for, in 1894, they were again on a collision course with the British. When a Royal Niger Company detachment under Lord Lugard arrived shortly before a French column at strategic and disputed Borgu near the Niger bend, war again became a distinct possibility. But cooler heads prevailed, mutual hostility was allayed, and the empire builders moved on, barely missing a beat. In the same year, the French reached Timbuktu. By 1896, the French tricolor flew over Say, on the Niger, and the Mossi lands in the Volta region. Futa Jallon in Guinea's interior was annexed shortly after. By 1900, an enormous land expanse had been taken, which included Senegal, the Ivory Coast, Dahomey, and French Guinea eastward to Lake Chad in the Sahara and north to Algeria, which would come to be known as French West Africa. Only the British conquest of the Sudan in 1898, the year of the Anglo-French agreement which settled many of the remaining contested territorial claims around the Niger, prevented the French empire from stretching unbroken from the Atlantic to the Red Sea.

The British, for their part, managed to crush and absorb the city-states of Ibadan (1893–95) and Abeokuta in 1893 and Benin in 1897. In Ashanti, the *asantehene* was destooled in 1896 and, after a brief but bloody revolt, Ashanti was attached to the Gold Coast colony in 1901. By 1906, the key Fulani political center of Sokoto, as well as Ilorin, Kano, Nupe, and Bornu, had felt the brunt of British imperialism as one by one they "accepted" protectorate status.

While border adjustments were still being made well into this century, all of Africa, with the exception of Liberia and Ethiopia, had been partitioned by 1914. Despite courageous yet futile resistance to European encroachment by the Ashanti, the Fulani, the Dahomeans, the Mauritanian Muslims, and many of the smaller Niger Delta tribes, the Europeans forged ahead and eventually all African opposition was leveled. The new colonies — makeshift entities created in Europe by drawing lines on inaccurate maps — split tribes, divided chiefdoms, and destroyed nations. Whatever political, economic, and social stability remained in West African society was disrupted to suit imperial purposes. When many of West Africa's colonial creations gained political independence in the 1950s and 1960s, tribal conflict erupted. The societies of these nations were far from homogeneous because of the method by which they were created. With the coming of independence, old quarrels and rivalries, suppressed by colonial governments, appeared once more. To be sure, other factors, economic as well as tribal — the recent Nigerian civil war being the most tragic example — enter into any explanation of West African instability. It cannot be denied, however, that the contemporary conflicts can be traced back to the earliest faltering European meddling in West African affairs, the culmination of which was the partition, rule, and exploitation of one continent by another.

CHAPTER SIX

European Colonialism and the Nationalist Challenge, 1914-1960

The time has really come for the Asiatics to govern themselves in Asia, as the Europeans are in Europe and the Western world, so also is it wise for the Africans to govern themselves at home, and thereby bring peace and satisfaction to the entire human family. — MARCUS GARVEY, 1923.[58]

BY 1914, THE IMPERIAL course in West Africa had been run. Along with most of the rest of Africa, it was now firmly in European hands. In the two decades preceding World War I, the imperialists set about organizing their territorial spoils into manageable administrative units. The Dutch, after transferring the last of their possessions to the British in the late nineteenth century, had disappeared from the West African scene. The Portuguese, once preeminent on the coast, retained but a toehold in West Africa. Only the tiny enclave of Portuguese Guinea, sandwiched between Senegal and French Guinea, served as a reminder of Portugal's long-lost West African empire. The Germans emerged from the Scramble with Kamerun (which later became the

Federal Republic of Cameroon) and Togoland. Their colonial reign was destined to be brief, however. After the war, under a mandate from the League of Nations, France and Great Britain divided Germany's West African colonies between them.

On the eve of war, Great Britain held Gambia, Sierra Leone, the Gold Coast, and Nigeria. Their colonial rival, France, was far and away the big winner in the imperial sweepstakes. Her colonial conquests, east and west, covered an area nearly twice America's land mass.

Each European power devised somewhat different methods for ruling its colonies. In Sierra Leone, the Niger Delta, the Gold Coast, and Gambia, where traditional systems of government had been undermined by the dual influences of Europeanization and urbanization, the British instituted direct rule. Where structured, traditional authority survived, as in Muslim-dominated Northern Nigeria, the British, through their governor-general Sir Frederick Lugard, practiced indirect rule. This meant simply that British authority supplemented traditional law and the native rulers—the chiefs and emirs—became agents through whom the British governed. On paper, indirect rule appeared workable. But when theory came up against reality and the British saw their interests threatened, they did not hesitate to intervene in the West African's affairs, time-honored traditions notwithstanding.

The West Indian-born black nationalist, George Padmore (1902–1959) took a dim view of what on the surface appeared to be Great Britain's imperial benevolence and concern for preserving native traditions. He claimed that "Indirect Rule is simply a cheap method of administering large tropical areas which would otherwise involve tremendous financial outlay to maintain a full-staffed white bureaucracy as in the case where Crown Colony, i.e. the Gold Coast or Direct Rule, obtains along the coast."[59]

Padmore's analysis of the motivation behind the indirect rule scheme came uncomfortably close to the mark. Throughout their tenure as colonial rulers, the British showed themselves to be pragmatic imperialists. West Africa had always been costly to administer. For centuries, the area had been known as "the white man's grave." Colonial service in West Africa was for many a life and death gamble until medical advances finally brought its widespread tropical diseases under control. East Africa, on the other hand, was strategically more important, more so after the opening of the Suez Canal, which shortened the trade route to the East. The promise of West Africa's valuable palm products, her groundnut crops, gold, rubber, and other useful exports, however, could not be ignored. During the nineteenth century, the British, as we have already mentioned, seriously considered withdrawing from West Africa. But the pressure applied by the established merchants and British financial and trading interests combined with international political considerations to lock them in. Like it or not, Great Britain would remain in West Africa until the tidal wave of nationalism and her own deteriorating world position made it impossible for her to maintain an overseas empire.

For the French in West Africa, the story was quite different. Like the British, they had been on the coast since the middle of the seventeenth century when French merchants opened trade at St. Louis in Senegal. In 1677, at about the same time the British entrenched themselves in Gambia, nearby Gorée was taken. While a special relationship between France and Senegal developed (Senegal sent deputies to the French Chamber of Deputies as early as 1848) it was only after the Scramble that the French set up an overall, centralized administration to govern their massive West African colonial domain.

In June 1895, a Government-General for West Africa was organized. First located at St. Louis in Senegal, it was shifted in 1904 to Dakar when the Federation of French West Africa was formed. Initially, French West Africa was composed of Senegal, French Guinea, the Ivory Coast, Dahomey, and an oversized territory known as Upper Senegal-Niger. It was France's hope that one day these possessions could be integrated into an intercontinental empire called Metropolitan France.

By 1920, territorial rearrangements and the bloody suppression by the French army of Muslim revolts in Niger, French Guinea, and Mauritania resulted in the reorganization of the French West African federation into eight colonies: Senegal,

French Guinea, the Ivory Coast, Haute or Upper
Volta (which was carved from the Upper Senegal-
Niger territory), Dahomey, Niger, Mauritania, and
French Soudan (Mali). This configuration remained
more or less stable until 1958 when, one by one,
France's colonies began to achieve their independ-
ence.

Rarely, if ever, did the French experiment with
indirect rule. Direct rule and centralization of authority were the cardinal principles of French colonialism in West Africa. Atop the governing pyramid
stood the colonial minister in Paris who dictated
policy to the governor-general in Dakar. It was
through the lieutenant-governors and their subordi-
nate commandants in each of the colonies that policy decisions were carried out. At the ground level,
chiefs and village headmen, responsible to the
French officials, were appointed. Virtually all aspects of the West African's life fell under the scruti-
ny of French officialdom. While a few West Africans — except for Senegal where there was comparatively substantial representation — sat on the practically powerless "advisory councils," they had little
voice in the running of the colony in which they
lived. Forced labor was not unusual and the majority
of West Africans were subject to a legal system
called the *indigénat*, under which, at a judge's request, they could be penalized and jailed without
trial for an unproven offense.

While the British did not make the anglicization
of the West African the keystone of their colonial

policy, the French did try to culturally assimilate their colonial subjects. According to her revolutionary constitution of 1892, French citizenship was theoretically extended to all subjects living under French sovereignty regardless of race. One of France's most cherished colonial objectives was to transform the African into a black Frenchman. For this purpose, French culture was imported into Africa and used as a tool to displace native institutions and traditions.

Assimilation worked best in Senegal, France's oldest West African colony, where there were a considerable number of black "citizens." However, for the West African roaming the deserts of Mauritania or living in Upper Volta's backwaters, assimilation was a word devoid of meaning. The Muslim populace, in particular, rebelled against France's tampering with its traditional ways and ties. For a brief while, the assimilation scheme was abandoned in favor of "association," a loosely defined plan aimed at educating an élite, which would be "associated" with the French life-style. Assimilation, however, survived association as an official colonial policy.

The Germans, before their ejection from Kamerun and Togoland, toyed with indirect rule, while the Portuguese adopted a French-style system of direct rule. Assimilation, too, was copied and made part of Portuguese colonial policy. Few Africans under Portuguese rule, however, ever achieved the coveted *assimilado* status for the requirements — a basic education and acceptability to the local Portuguese functionary—were and are still insurmountable obstacles.

These, then, were the alien forms of government imposed upon the West African in his native land and which, from their inception, became the target of the African nationalist.

The historian Colin Legum has defined nationalism as a political force which promotes the idea of a nation and which mobilizes mass support to transform this idea into reality. Nationalism, therefore, can exist—and usually does—even before the nation itself. African nationalism is perhaps as old as Africa. It certainly was not a phenomenon unique to the nineteenth and twentieth centuries. Nationalism was present in the days of Sunni Ali and no doubt in earlier times. Often, when one African nation was threatened by another or, later, by European nations, nationalism—that mystical sense of community and tribal identity—served as a call to arms. West Africa's history is filled with examples of nationalist reaction to external threats: Sunni Ali's crushing of the Muslims, the Ashanti stand against the British, the Dahomeans' running battle with the French, and the Fanti's opposition to the Ashanti and their own admirable though futile effort to create a nationalist confederation in the late nineteenth century.

Ironically, many West African nationalists of the nineteenth and twentieth centuries were products of universities in the same European nations that ruled their homelands. They returned home from their studies abroad, brimming with the ideals of European humanism, and set about turning their acquired beliefs into actuality. George Osokele Johnson (1825?–1899), an Egba, consistently fought against the extension of British rule in his native Nigeria while James Africanus Horton (1835–1882), a Sierra Leonean physician and graduate of the University of Edinburgh, appeared before Parliament in 1865 to urge support for the creation of an independent Fanti nation. While the Fanti confederation, as we know, foundered on the shoals of British suspicions, Horton continued to advocate the cause of African independence and racial equality.

Samuel Lewis (1843–1903), a Sierra Leonean Creole, became a barrister in 1872. Knighted by Queen Victoria in 1893, his life was one long struggle on behalf of his countrymen, from defending their civil rights to working for more native representation on the Sierra Leonean governing bodies.

Edward Wilmot Blyden (1832–1912), another nineteenth-century nationalist, was born on the island of St. Thomas in the West Indies. He lived in the United States for a number of years where, burned by racism and prejudice, he became convinced that only in Africa could the black man achieve equality and rekindle the singular genius he believed was inherent in the black race. In 1851, Edward Blyden emigrated to Liberia. A scholar fluent in many European languages, he served Liberia in many official capacities during his long career.

The American-born and Harvard-educated nationalist, Martin R. Delany (1812–1885), visited Africa in the 1850s as part of a commission sponsored by a Cleveland-based emigration society. Like Blyden and Horton, Delany strongly supported an African-ruled Africa, emphasizing that "the claims of no people are respected by any nation until they are presented in a national capacity."[60]

These isolated voices of African nationalism, of an "Africa for Africans," became legion as the nineteenth century drew to a close. In 1897, when the British attempted to exploit the Gold Coast's palm forests at the expense of its native inhabitants, a Ghanaian barrister, J. E. Casely Hayford (1866–1930), organized the Aborigines Rights' Protection Society to oppose the move. Under Hayford's leadership, the ARPS managed to force the colonial government to back down.

After the signal success of the ARPS, the pioneer nationalists began to realize that their only hope of drawing concessions from the West African colonial governments was through concerted efforts. With this in mind, the first Pan-African Conference met in London in 1900, its avowed aim to promote solidarity among the world's "colored races."

Among the American delegates to the historic meeting was W. E. B. DuBois (1868–1963), the brilliant Massachusetts-born and Harvard-trained black scholar, author, and later founder of the National Association for the Advancement of Colored People. DuBois, through his persuasive writings and his very presence, would exert the greatest spiritual and intellectual influence on the growth of African nationalism. DuBois, a prophet rejected by his own countrymen, a man persecuted throughout his life for his politics, unerringly prophesied seventy years ago that the "problem of the twentieth century is the problem of the color line." His lifelong belief in and espousal of the cause of African nationalism and freedom would be justified when in 1957 Ghana became black Africa's first nation to cast off the bonds of colonialism.

In 1961, in despair over an America torn by racial conflict, DuBois left the United States for Ghana, where he soon after became a citizen. On August 27, 1963, W. E. B. DuBois died in Accra at the age of 95.

World War I gave West African nationalism a boost. The Senegalese rifleman fought beside the British West African and American soldier on the European battlefields. After the war, when each returned home, the West African, whose blood had been spilled on behalf of his colonial master, realized more than ever that he was being short-changed and determined to do something about it. Nationalist opinion began to focus.

In 1919, to coincide with the Versailles Conference, black leaders, led by Senegal's Blaise Diagne (1872–1934) and DuBois, gathered in Paris, intent on bringing the problems of the black man before the councils of world opinion. This Pan-African Conference presented modest demands by today's standards — protection for the Africans, improved labor conditions, and an end to the colonialists' exploitation of African resources.

Unfortunately, dissension among the representatives was rife. Diagne, once a radical nationalist who early in his career attacked the abuses of French rule in his native Senegal, had by this time become an apologist for French policies in West Africa. The first African ever to represent Senegal in the French Chamber of Deputies, he opposed any criticism of French colonial policy. At odds with DuBois, Diagne proved a divisive element in a movement which desperately needed unity to survive. Without the wholehearted support of influential Africans like Diagne, the Pan-African movement could never amount to more than an ineffectual debating society.

In 1920, another nationalist group, the National Congress of British West Africa, under Casely Hayford's guidance, convened in London. The Congress put the British on notice that the West African would no longer accept the colonial status quo. The NCBWA did succeed in precipitating changes in the character and form of British rule. In 1922, Nigeria became the first of Great Britain's West African colonies to permit the election of Africans to its legislative council. The reforms in Nigeria and in Great Britain's other West African possessions were small but they clearly signified a crack in the colonial monolith. The British had at last decided to listen.

While DuBois and others were promoting the cause of Pan-Africanism and nationalism, Jamaican-born Marcus Aurelius Garvey (1887–1940) began to preach his doctrines of racial separation and black pride, urging Americans of African descent to return to Africa. In 1914, Garvey constructed the vehicle through which he would propagate his views, the Universal Negro Improvement Association. In 1920, the Harlem-based UNIA sponsored an international convention, which was attended by many of the world's black dignitaries, including the mayor of Monrovia, Liberia. The convention predictably elected Garvey Provisional President of Africa.

Garvey's organization by this time boasted a shipping line, a military wing called the Universal African Legion, a newspaper, a corps of black nurses, and the African Orthodox Church where Garvey's followers worshipped a black Madonna and a black Christ.

Unfortunately, Garvey's "back to Africa" program and his belief in racial segregation attracted support from America's lunatic fringe—the Ku Klux Klan and other white supremacist groups—all of whom favored his repatriation schemes. At the same time, Garvey's activities and his considerable success in arousing America's black populace against the injustices of America's institutionalized racism alarmed the United States government. It soon launched an investigation into the UNIA's financial operations, which proved to be as unorthodox as Garvey himself. In 1925, he was indicted on a charge of mail fraud, tried, convicted, and deported. In 1940, Marcus Garvey died in London.

Despite his questionable financial dealings, Garvey's ability to instill in thousands a pride in their black heritage stands as his greatest and most enduring accomplishment. To his dying day, he kept the faith that "Africa must be redeemed" for, Garvey insisted, "if Europe is for the Europeans then Africa shall be for the black peoples of the world."

During the early years of the depression-ridden thirties, nationalism suffered severe setbacks. Financial contributions lagged and many nationalist movements ceased to exist. The collapse of the National Congress of British West Africa followed the death of Casely Hayford in 1930. The Pan-Africanists, too, were in economic straits. In French West Africa, the colonial government's "get tough" policy hampered nationalist activities. Yet, even in the midst of worldwide economic dislocation, nationalism in West Africa underwent a transformation. By the mid-thirties, its ranks were slowly increased and its base broadened. Clandestine labor unions, drawing their numbers from the workers who flooded West Africa's cities in search of employment, played a major role in nationalism's resurgence. The nationalist leadership was no longer the exclusive province of the European-educated intellectual élite. The labor unions produced Siaka Stevens, Sierra Leone's president and his Guinean counterpart, Sékou Touré (b. 1922), a descendant of the nineteenth-century warrior Samori Touré.

To complement the labor movement, tribal and youth groups were chartered. In British West Africa, the most notable of these were the West African Students' Union, the Nigerian Youth Movement in which the Nigerian statesman Nnamdi Azikiwe (b. 1904), the son of a military clerk, served his nationalist apprenticeship, Sierra Leonean Wallace Johnson's West African Youth League, and Dr. J. B. Danquah's Gold Coast Youth Conference. These small, nearly penniless organizations, filled with idealistic young nationalists, became a spawning ground for the future leaders of an independent West Africa.

For the West African, World War II was, in a sense, a replay of World War I. Again he answered the colonialist's call, fought bravely, and came back to a homeland little changed from the one he had left a few years before. Yet this time his return was marked by a far more drastic change in attitude. Pleas for reform were replaced by unequivocal demands for self-government. The British West African pressed his colonial overseer to make good on his wartime declarations of freedom and equality. For the black African, these basic human rights could no longer be reserved for the white European: he demanded they be extended to him and his black brothers.

On October 15, 1945, the fifth and most significant Pan-African Conference opened in Manchester, England. Its delegates' list read like a Who's Who in African nationalism. Taking part were Kwame Nkrumah of the Gold Coast, the West Indian nationalist George Padmore, Kenya's Jomo Kenyatta, Sierra Leone's Wallace Johnson, and, of course, the ageless W. E. B. DuBois. When the gathering disbanded, the colonial powers realized that the West African freedom movement had passed the point of no return. The demands for independence and autonomy voiced at the conference would have to be heeded. Time and circumstance were at last on the nationalists' side.

In post-war Great Britain, a Labour government had just been installed, more disposed to sympathize with the nationalists' position. The fact that India, the jewel of Great Britain's Eastern empire, had been scheduled for independence was not lost on the nationalists. In West Africa the fires of discontent flared, fanned by the impatience of a younger generation of students, workers, and intellectuals unwilling to accept crumbs from the colonial table. For this new African, schooled in European universities, hardened on the European battlefield, and with world opinion swinging in his favor, the myth of European superiority was dead. It was replaced by a self-confidence and an awareness of his African identity. The time for retrieving his birthright—his native land—had arrived.

Agitation for self-government swept West Africa by the late forties. In the Gold Coast, J. B. Danquah's youth movement had evolved into a political party called the United Gold Coast Convention (UGCC). Danquah's secretary was American-educated Kwame Nkrumah (b. 1909). An intimate of George Padmore whose writings, along with those of W. E. B. DuBois, helped shape his nationalist philosophy, Nkrumah studied at both Lincoln and Pennsylvania universities before returning to the Gold Coast after the war. In 1948, he spearheaded the boycott against Accra's Syrian and European merchants who were taking advantage of post-war food shortages to charge the African exorbitant prices. The riots that grew out of the boycott caused the arrest of both Danquah and Nkrumah. The British commission of inquiry, which investigated the disturbances, merely underlined what everybody already knew were the prime causes for the rising: the miserable conditions awaiting the returning soldiers as well as the feeling of frustration among the educated Africans.

After his release from jail, Nkrumah decided to break away from the comparatively moderate Danquah and form his own party. In 1949, with other militant Gold Coast nationalists, he formed the Convention People's Party (CPP).

At about the same time, the British, who had already accepted the inevitability of self-government and eventual independence for its West African colonies, planned to introduce a new constitution in the Gold Coast. This document increased the number of Africans on the colony's law-making body, the legislative council. Nkrumah considered this woefully inadequate and he increased the pressure for self-government by calling for strikes. In 1950, Nkrumah was again imprisoned, this time for sedition. In February 1951, national elections were held in the Gold Coast and the CPP won a smashing victory. The embarrassed colonial government had little choice but to free Nkrumah, the party's volatile leader.

After his release in 1951, Kwame Nkrumah effectively consolidated his power within the CPP. In 1952, he became Prime Minister of the colony and two years later, the Gold Coast was granted internal self-government. Finally, on March 6, 1957, with Kwame Nkrumah at its helm, the Gold Coast accomplished its long awaited goal—independence from Great Britain. After this momentous event, the new nation changed its European name to Ghana, after the ancient empire which flourished nearly a thousand years before.

Ghana was but a beginning. In Nigeria, nationalism also smoldered just beneath the surface and, as in Ghana, burst forth after the war. Its foremost leader was Nnamdi Azikiwe. Like Nkrumah, Azikiwe, or "Zik" as he is popularly known, studied at Lincoln University. A member of the Nigerian Youth Movement in the thirties, he later served as an aide to Herbert Macaulay, head of the nationalist group, the Nigerian National Council. He succeeded to the organization's presidency after Macaulay's death in 1946, renaming it the National Council of

Nigeria and the Cameroons (NCNC). In the same year, Great Britain divided Nigeria into three regions, each of which was representative of one of Nigeria's three major tribal and religious groupings. The Northern region, as we have noted, was Muslim-dominated; the Western region, including the city of Lagos, had a Yoruba majority; and the Eastern region, where Azikiwe enjoyed his largest following, was the home of the Ibo peoples.

While Ghana had its domestic problems, these were dwarfed by the staggering tribal differences with which Nigeria was, and is still today, saddled. Azikiwe's NCNC was Ibo-controlled, which made it suspect in the eyes of the northern Muslims. Consequently, a second political party, the Northern People's Congress (NPC) was formed, under the direction of the Sardauna of Sokoto, Sir Ahmadu Bello. In the west, Obafemi Awolowo, a Yoruba chief, who like Azikiwe once belonged to the Nigerian Youth Movement, founded in 1951 yet another political force, the Action Group of Western Nigeria. Each party represented Nigeria's conflicting religious, tribal, and economic interests, an unhealthy situation which kept them at odds with one another and culminated two decades later in the Nigerian civil war.

It was not unusual, given the circumstances, that the 1950s in Nigeria were marked by uncertainty and tensions. As in Ghana and Sierra Leone, the British permitted greater self-government, optimistic that Nigeria's sharp regional rivalries might somehow be muted under a federal form of government. In 1954, a federal system was introduced and by 1959, when each of Nigeria's three regions had become self-governing, nationwide elections were held. Nigerians voted along regional (and therefore tribal) lines and Ahmadu Bello's Northern People's Congress, in a coalition with the NCNC, scored a victory. The party named Abubakar Tafawa Balewa to fill the office of Prime Minister in the new government. Azikiwe, whose NCNC ran second, became President of the Nigerian senate. A free Nigeria was about to be born. On October 1, 1960, she became the second British West African colony to achieve independence.

By 1965, Sierra Leone and Gambia had joined Ghana and Nigeria in freedom. British West Africa thus quietly passed into history as four sovereign West African nations took its place.

Whereas the British accepted the inevitability of independence for their West African colonies, the French, until almost the last moment, steadfastly refused to face the possibility. They promoted the myth of Metropolitan France, peopled by black Frenchmen loyal to the self-appointed "mother country," France herself. The French ideal was shared by few of her West African subjects.

The late twenties and thirties in French West Africa were as difficult a time for the nationalists as for their brothers in British West Africa. But, as in British West Africa, the nationalists tenaciously held their ground and added to their numbers. As London and America bred British West Africa's nationalists, so too did Paris serve the same function for French Africa's anti-colonialists. Nationalist sentiments were being voiced by many French-speaking Africans in both Europe and Africa during this period. A Dahomean journalist, Louis Hunkanrin, edited a newspaper in Paris which exposed and protested against the conditions in his French-ruled homeland. Léopold Sédar Senghor (b. 1907), the poet-president of Senegal, agitated in behalf of self-government. His protégé, Lamine Gueye, the first French-speaking African to be awarded a Doctor of Laws degree from the Sorbonne, joined with Senegal's European socialists to form the Senegalese Socialist Party. In French Guinea, a nationalist movement called the Voice of the Highlanders evolved into the Guinean Socialist Party. In Guinea, too, Sékou Touré became a central figure in his nation's labor struggle.

Nationalism in French West Africa was growing quickly when the war overtook the world. During World War II, the French-speaking African's contributions paralleled those of his English-speaking West African neighbors.

Even before General Charles DeGaulle's Free French Army liberated Paris in 1944, France's post-war colonial policy was being charted at Brazzaville in the French Congo. The conference decided to increase African representation to the French Chamber of Deputies, to replace the terms "colony" with "overseas territory," and French "Empire" with

French "Union." The hated *indigénat* and forced labor were both abolished. But the dream of a Metropolitan France lingered. Despite the surge of nationalist fervor in Great Britain's African colonies, independence for France's colonial territories was not considered by her to be even a distant prospect.

In French West Africa, as in British West Africa, the atmosphere had indeed changed. Many French-speaking Africans rejected the future as defined for them at Brazzaville. In 1946, French Africa's black leaders met at Bamako in the French Soudan where they founded Africa's first inter-territorial political party, the Rassemblement Démocratique Africain (RDA). Its leader was the highly respected French-trained physician and parliamentary deputy from the Ivory Coast, Félix Houphouët-Boigny.

Allying itself with the French Communist Party (1946–1950), the RDA demanded immediate equality for France's colonial subjects. In those formative years, the RDA benefited greatly from the Communists' proven organizing ability, a skill used by Houphouët for the RDA's own purposes. The Senegalese socialists, Léopold Senghor and Lamine Gueye, chose not to join the RDA, preferring instead to pursue their own, at that time more moderate, brand of nationalism. This breach in nationalist thought and policy was the first sign that the RDA would never become an umbrella under which nationalists of all persuasions would be comfortable.

In 1947, Senghor and the poets Alioun Diop and Aimé Césaire published the first issue of the influential cultural review, *Présence Africaine*. The journal enjoyed the sponsorship of French intellectuals Jean-Paul Sartre, Albert Camus, and André Gide, and the American author Richard Wright. The concept of *négritude*, the sense of identity or consciousness in being black, was promoted in the pages of *Présence Africaine* and soon developed into as profound a political and intellectual philosophy as Pan-Africanism. *Négritude*, however, has had its detractors. Guinea's Sékou Touré has attacked its basic premises. At the 1969 Pan-African cultural festival held in Algiers, he said that "there is no black culture, nor white culture, nor yellow culture," and concluded that "Négritude is thus a false concept, an irrational weapon encouraging the irrationality based on racial discrimination, arbitrarily exercised upon the peoples of Africa, Asia and upon men of color in America and Europe."

In 1947, Senghor and Lamine Gueye had a falling out. Senghor subsequently brought his Senegalese followers together in the Bloc Démocratique Sénégalais (BDS). Almost simultaneously, Senghor widened the rift between himself and Houphouët by raising a still larger inter-territorial political group, the Indépendants d'Outre-Mer (IOM).

By 1950, the complexion of the RDA had begun to change. Its beginnings and many of its early political positions had been progressive and promising. But, like the UGCC in the Gold Coast, it had become more conservative. With its increasing conservatism it became more acceptable to France's colonial ministry, especially after it broke with the

French Communist Party. While the party was unable to control its more independently minded Cameroon and Niger sections, both of which defected from the parent group, it did manage to stave off a serious political challenge in the early 1950s by the now more militant IOM. The RDA even recouped much of its political leverage by the middle of the decade, thanks to Houphouët's diplomatic talents and French support.

As a colonial power, France's reach, by the middle of the twentieth century, far exceeded her grasp. Her imperial dream had become a nightmare as she found herself fighting a losing battle against nationalist movements on many fronts. French power was in rapid decline, accelerated by her involvement in the Indochinese quagmire and the seemingly endless Algerian War. The Suez Crisis of 1956 shook France even more. Weakened by futile military adventures abroad and political and economic chaos at home, France found herself being ripped apart. As it turned out, 1956 was for her a year of critical decisions which had tremendous repercussions south of the Sahara. Morocco and Tunisia were given their independence and a new colonial statute, the *loi-cadre* or Outline Law was enacted. The federations of French West and French Equatorial Africa were abolished and a streamlined, decentralized, and more representative system replaced them. Along with centralization, another keystone of France's cultural colonialism was abandoned—the time-worn policy of assimilation.

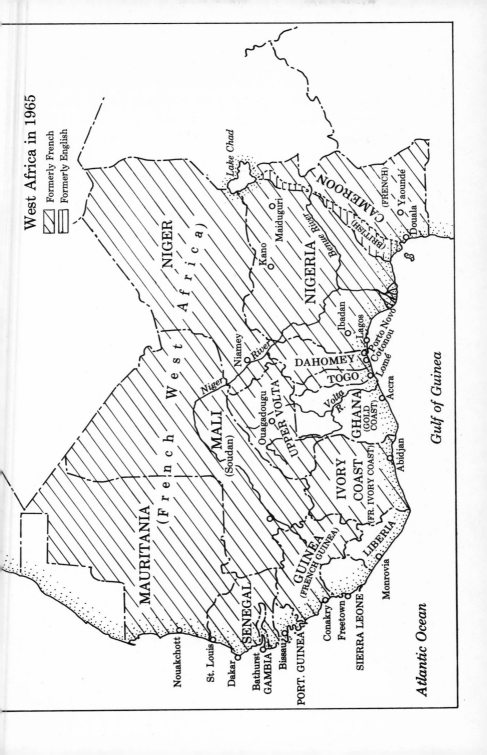

West Africa in 1965

Formerly French
Formerly English

Atlantic Ocean

Gulf of Guinea

Nouakchott

St. Louis

Dakar

Bathurst
GAMBIA
Bissau
PORT. GUINEA

Conakry
Freetown

SIERRA LEONE

Monrovia

MAURITANIA

(French West Africa)

SENEGAL

GUINEA
(FRENCH GUINEA)

LIBERIA

MALI
(Soudan)

Niger River

Niamey

Ouagadougou

UPPER VOLTA

IVORY
COAST
(FR. IVORY COAST)

Abidjan

NIGER

Lake Chad

Kano

Maiduguri

NIGERIA

Ibadan

Lagos

Porto Novo
Cotonou

DAHOMEY

TOGO

Lomé

Accra

GHANA
(GOLD
COAST)

Volta R.

Benue River

CAMEROON
(BRITISH)

(FRENCH)

Yaoundé

Douala

The *loi cadre* did little to unify or pacify the nationalists, however. At the RDA's Bamako Conference of 1957, factionalism increased. Both Sékou Touré and Léopold Senghor viewed the new colonial code as divisive. They saw as its aim the weakening of the nationalist movements of every stripe through the "balkanizing" of the French West and Equatorial African territories. Houphouët-Boigny disagreed and supported the French plan. After Bamako, Touré and Modibo Keita of the French Soudan broke with the RDA once and for all and formed the opposition Parti du Régroupement Africain (PRA) On the eve of independence, nationalism in French West Africa was still divided.

The Suez debacle and the Algerian War's fatal drain on France's manpower and her economy had France's Fourth Republic, by 1958, teetering on the edge of collapse. The star of General Charles De-Gaulle, in abeyance since his brief term as France's post-war president, was on the rise once more. Called out of retirement in June, he agreed to assume the presidency of France's ministerial council. One of his first official acts was to offer French Africa a constitutional referendum by which it could choose independence or self-government within a French Community (resembling the British Commonwealth) with DeGaulle at its head. Houphouët-Boigny counseled in favor of ratifying the constitution. Only Sékou Touré urged immediate independence.

Aware of Touré's stance, DeGaulle stated that "independence is available to Guinea; she can have it; she can have it on 28 September by voting 'no' to the proposition that is put to her, and in saying this I guarantee that Paris will raise no obstacle to it." Touré replied that "we prefer poverty in freedom to riches in slavery." Touré's action proved decisive. Guinea's opting for independence proved lethal to the French Community. In response, De Gaulle angrily ordered the immediate removal of French technicians and halted financial assistance to Guinea. But DeGaulle found that it was too late for threats. One by one, France's African possessions followed Guinea's example.

In April 1960, French Togoland (British Togoland joined Ghana after a plebescite in 1956) became the Republic of Togo. The Northern and Southern Cameroons, the United Nations trusteeships inherited from the defunct League of Nations, gained their independence. The Northern Cameroons attached itself to Nigeria while the Southern Cameroons was absorbed into the Federal Republic of Cameroon. The brittle structure of DeGaulle's grand French Community thus buckled and came crashing to earth.

When the British withdrew from Gambia in 1965, West Africa, with the exception of Portuguese Guinea, was liberated from a European rule begun five centuries before when Gil Eanne's caravel first dropped anchor off the West African coast.

CHAPTER SEVEN

Biafra:
Imperialism's Legacy

Nigeria never was and can never be a united country. — GENERAL C. ODUMEGWU OJUKWU, former leader of the Republic of Biafra, 1969.[61]

Our objective was to crush the rebellion, to maintain the territorial integrity of our nation, to assert the ability of the black man to build a strong, progressive, and prosperous modern nation. — MAJOR-GENERAL YAKUBU GOWON, head of the Federal Military Government of Nigeria, January 13, 1970.[62]

ON JANUARY 12, 1970, Major-General Philip Effiong, Odumegwu Ojukwu's successor as head of the moribund Republic of Biafra, issued the following statement:

> It is my sincere hope the lessons of the bitter struggle have been well learned by everybody and I would like therefore to take this opportunity to say that I, Major-General Philip Effiong, officer administering the government of the Republic of Biafra, now wish to make the following declaration:
>
> That we are firm, we are loyal Nigerian citizens and accept the authority of the federal military government of Nigeria.

That we accept the existing administrative and political structure of the Federation of Nigeria.

That the Republic of Biafra hereby ceases to exist.[63]

Thus the curtain came down on the briefly independent Republic of Biafra. The Nigerian civil war was at an end.

The shooting war actually began a month after Biafra's secession on May 30, 1967, but its root cause goes back much earlier. The destructive forces the conflict released were the logical consequence of the actions taken by the European powers during imperialism's heyday—the late nineteenth century. As Africa was being mindlessly carved up among the colonialists, Great Britain accumulated, through the device of "protectorates," what later came to be called Nigeria. In 1914, as has been mentioned, the British amalgamated their various "protectorates" and pieced together the Colony and Protectorate of Nigeria.

Nigeria is today, as it was in 1914, a conglomeration of more than 250 tribes. The largest of these are the Hausa-Fulani of the North, the Yoruba in the West and Mid-West, and the Ibo of the Eastern Region. The Hausa-Fulani are descendants of the Muslim faithful who rallied around Uthman dan Fodio and his Islamic revolution during the early nineteenth century. They are conservative and, in many respects, their life style is feudal. By way of contrast, the Yoruba and even more so, the Ibo, are Westernized peoples noted for progressive political and social attitudes, many of which are thoroughly alien to their Hausa neighbors. The British, during their colonial reign, managed to keep an uneasy peace among these ethnic groups.

As we know, on October 1, 1960, after years of nationalist agitation, Nigeria gained her independence. Soon after, the old antagonisms in this culturally diverse nation of 55 millions bubbled to the surface. To most Nigerians, these hostilities came as no surprise. They may have been muted under British rule, but their presence was always recognized. In 1947, the Yoruba chief, Obafemi Awolowo, had written:

> Nigeria is not a nation. It is a mere geographical expression. There are no "Nigerians" in the same sense as there are "English," "Welsh," or "French." The word "Nigerian" is merely a distinctive appellation to distinguish those who live within the boundaries of Nigeria from those who do not.[55]

As time passed, Nigeria more and more fit Awolowo's description. By the time she declared herself a federal republic on October 1, 1963, public outrage and criticism of widespread government corruption was becoming more frequent. The storm warnings were up. The government, however, failed to heed them.

When the Western Region's premier, Chief Samuel Akintola, jailed the highly respected Chief Awolowo on treason charges in 1963 and, two years later, rigged the regional elections (with the tacit support of the Northern Region's Muslim premier, Sir Ahmadu Bello), Nigeria was shaken to its founda-

tions. Democracy's future in the nation which everyone considered the linchpin of a stable, independent
Africa was in doubt. Nigeria, it was now clear, was a
nation unified only on paper.

The Akintola-Bello axis marked the end of Nigeria's fragile unity of compromise. On January 15,
1966, disgruntled Ibo officers rebelled and murdered Sir Ahmadu Bello, Chief Samuel Akintola,
Nigeria's Prime Minister, Sir Abubakar Tafawa
Balewa, and the key army officers from the North and
West. In the aftermath of this bloodshed, Major-
General J. T. U. Aguiyi-Ironsi assumed control of
the federal government. During his seven months in
office, Ironsi, an Ibo, rotated Hausa military units
and approved the promotion of a disproportionate
number of Ibo officers in order to insure Ibo securi-
ty. These moves alarmed the many non-Ibos in the
officers' corps. On July 29, Ironsi's regime came to
an abrupt end when the general and two hundred
Eastern officers were killed by Hausa soldiers.

With Ironsi gone, Ibo influence began to fade.
Colonel Yakubu Gowon stepped in to head Nigeria's military government. Gowon, who was born in
the Northern Region, was neither Ibo nor Hausa
but a Christian from a minor tribe whose tribal cre-
dentials were acceptable to both warring camps. By
the time Gowon took over, however, anti-Ibo feeling in the Northern Region had already reached a
high pitch. There was little Gowon could do to prevent the inevitable Ibo-Hausa confrontation.

Many thousands of Ibos, unable to prosper or use

their talents as technicians, clerks, professionals, and
businessmen in their native Eastern Region, had
emigrated and settled in Nigeria's north and west.
There they prospered and, when they could, assisted
other Ibos. Ibo aggressiveness, frankness, and what
some have termed "arrogance," did little to endear
these industrious people to their non-Ibo compatriots. James Africanus Horton, the nineteenth-century African nationalist born of Ibo parents in Sierra
Leone, commented:

> The Egboes [Ibo] are considered the most imitative
> and emulative people in the whole of Western Africa;
> place them where you will, or introduce them to any
> manners and customs, you will find that they very easily
> adapt themselves to them. Stout-hearted, or, to use the
> more common phraseology, big-hearted, they always pos-
> sess a desire of superiority, and make attempts to attain
> it, or excel in what is praiseworthy, without a desire of
> depressing others. To them we may well apply the lan-
> guage of Dryden: "A noble emulation beats their
> breasts." Place an Egboe [Ibo] man in a comfortable posi-
> tion, and he will never rest satisfied until he sees others
> occupying the same or a similar position.[64]

The rising tide of hate exploded again in September 1966. For the Ibo, the bloodbath had begun. An
estimated thirty thousand Ibos died during these
riots and, before it was over, most of the Ibos living
in the Muslim-populated Northern Region fled eastward.

As Yakubu Gowon's military governor for the
Eastern Region, Lieutenant-Colonel Odumegwu
Ojukwu had first counseled in favor of reconcilia-

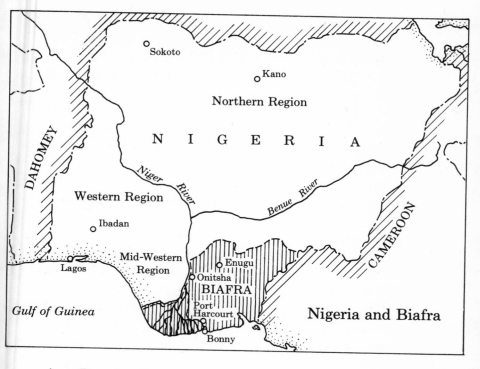

Nigeria and Biafra

tion. But the September massacre, with its very real prospect of Ibo extermination, along with Gowon's unwillingness to grant Ibo demands for greater home rule, made secession inevitable. Between September 1966 and Ojukwu's declaration of Biafran independence in May 1967, the groundwork for secession was laid. The Eastern Region withheld payment of taxes to the Federal Military Government in Lagos, non-Easterners were deported, and Ojukwu pursued a policy of active non-cooperation in dealing with Gowon.

The Eastern Region, renamed the Republic of Biafra was, in May 1967, roughly the size of Connecticut. Nine million Ibo lived among its population of fifteen millions. The remaining six million Biafrans were members of the Efik, Ibibio, Ijaw, and Ogoja tribes. Few of these peoples had great affection for the Ibos, who were in the majority. Three-fourths of Nigeria's lucrative oil deposits lay in the non-Ibo areas within the Eastern Region. Colonel Ojukwu counted upon these resources to see his embryonic nation through the uncertain days ahead.

The minority Biafrans soon learned that self-determination was an Ibo concept, and political and physical harassment were not practiced exclusively by the Muslim Hausa or the Gowon government. When an Ibibio, Efik, Ijaw, or Ogojo failed to comply with the wishes of the Ibo majority, brute force was often used against him. Biafran unity was as much a figment of the imagination as was the once-heralded Nigerian unity.

On May 27, 1967, three days before the Biafran secession, General Gowon divided Nigeria into twelve states, three of which were in the Eastern Region. Two of the three new states were reserved for the minority tribes in an obvious effort to undercut the Ibo position and drive a greater wedge between the Ibo secessionists and the minority tribes. Gowon's geographic shuffling failed to weaken the Ibo resolve and, in early July, civil war came to Nigeria.

From the very beginning, Biafra was clearly out-

matched. Its army lacked the training, the equip-
ment, and the international support that Nigeria's
army had. Only the Ivory Coast, Tanzania, Zambia,
Gabon, and Haiti recognized the breakaway state.
France, perhaps in return for mineral concessions,
covertly favored the Biafrans, and Portugal, in her
never-ending quest for African allies, channeled aid
and arms to Biafra through the Gulf of Guinea island of Fernando Po. Great Britain, a heavy investor
in Nigeria's economy, and the Soviet Union, seeking to gain a firmer foothold in West Africa, backed
the Gowon government. The United States stayed
neutral, placing an embargo on arms sales to both
sides.

The Nigerian military government banked on an
easy and swift victory. It successfully blockaded
Biafra's ports and placed her under virtual siege.
Gowon, however, had underestimated the tenacity
of the Biafrans. Still, Biafra's cause was clearly hopeless and, through 1968, deaths, due mostly to starvation, increased rapidly. As the horrors of the war
were splashed in headlines and on television around
the world, international pressure for a settlement of
the conflict intensified.

In May 1968, tentative peace discussions opened
in Kampala, Uganda. No headway was made, for the
Ojukwu regime insisted on a cease-fire before talks
could begin, while the Lagos government's representatives demanded an end to the Biafran secession
as a prerequisite to the cease-fire. The diplomatic
logjam continued at Niamey (Niger) in July and at

Addis Ababa (Ethiopia) in August. A "mercy corridor," offered by Nigeria as a conduit through which food could be supplied to the starving Biafrans, was rejected by Ojukwu, who feared that these life-saving supplies might be poisoned. The war dragged on, and the hopeless look on the faces of dying Biafran men, women, and children was by now a dishearteningly familiar sight.

Although their beleaguered nation was shrinking daily in both size and population, the Biafrans persisted. Yet, despite a sustained drive by Biafran forces in April 1969, Federal troops frequently met only scattered opposition as the year wore on. By September, it became clear that Biafra was in its death throes. Her cities and ports had fallen in quick succession, her army had been decimated, and the will of her people to continue the fight had disappeared. Finally, on January 10, 1970, Biafra's commander-in-chief, Odumegwu Ojukwu, took flight. The Biafran experiment had failed.

In a civil war there are no victors. The Nigerian conflict was no exception. Human losses, over two million by most estimates, were staggering. The oil refineries of Nigeria can always be rebuilt, but the destruction of the human spirit, the psychological damage inflicted upon all the Nigerian peoples by the war, may never be repaired.

CHAPTER EIGHT

West Africa: A Decade of Independence

Our voice booms across the oceans and mountains, over the hills and valleys, in the desert places and through the vast expanse of mankind's habitation, and calls out for the freedom of Africa; Africa wants her freedom; Africa must be free. — KWAME NKRUMAH, 1960.[65]

AS THE 1950s waned, Africa's nations, along with others in the newly independent "Third World," underwent changes of great magnitude. Shifts in political affiliations and in attitudes toward former colonial overlords began to take place. Too long had Africa — north, south, east, and west — labored under colonialism's thumb. Heeding the immortal advice that "eternal vigilance is the price of liberty," the young African states committed themselves to the defense of their hard-won freedom by actively opposing efforts by their former masters to manipulate their destiny in the many guises of neo-colonialism. When the sixties ended, Africa's leaders had, for the most part, steered an unnerving course between the Scylla and Charybdis of Western capitalism and Eastern socialism with all the dangers this non-alignment entailed.

199

More often than not, these leaders acted in what they considered the best interests of their nations. Often they were forced to play the game of pitting one superpower against another. With alarming frequency, too, many of Africa's leaders fell victim to the murderous internal politics characteristic of artificially created nations cursed with irreconcilable interests and heterogeneous populations with only long-standing enmities in common.

With the cards stacked against them, these nations somehow endured the internal and external buffeting and retained their sovereignty. Many have not prospered and have, in fact, regressed economically and politically. Others have been torn by war. Yet each of Africa's independent states has managed to survive their most crucial first decade intact.

The early years of independence were notable for a proliferation of inter-continental conferences and quasi-alliances. Most of all, however, they were marked by the emergence of Kwame Nkrumah. As Africa's most dynamic personality, Nkrumah dominated many of these conferences and alliances. In Cairo (1957), the first of the African-based gatherings, at the Nkrumah-sponsored Conference of Independent African States (1958), and the All-African Peoples Conference (1958) in Accra, and later Conakry (1960), the former Ghanaian president repeatedly stressed the dangers of neo-colonialism. With Suez a recent, painful memory, the Congo disaster coming hard on the heels of the Algerian War, and the French decision to conduct nuclear tests in the

Sahara, it is easy to understand why the fear of neo-colonialism often obscured many of Africa's other pressing problems. This fear was exploited by Nkrumah as he sought to unite Africa politically and thereby turn the Pan-African dream into a reality.

Nkrumah was unsuccessful and his failure was the failure of every political giant who becomes a prisoner of his own grandiose and impossible schemes. But, for a time, he brought to a young Africa prestige and respect and provided Pan-Africanism with a vocal, articulate world leader unafraid to state his views and act upon them.

Nkrumah's first step toward a centralized Africa was his formation of a union with Sékou Touré's Guinea in November 1958. Resource-blessed Ghana and economically crippled Guinea proved strange bedfellows. The showcase union was loosely constructed and badly planned, plagued from its inception by different economies, currencies, and languages.

The Ghana-Guinea Union soon had its counterpart elsewhere in West Africa. In April 1959, the former French Soudan of Modibo Keita and Léopold Senghor's Senegal emerged as the Federation of Mali. Unfortunately, it died, by August 1960, as charges and countercharges of usurpation of power and plotting were leveled at each other by Senghor and Keita.

After the Mali Federation's disintegration, Senegal went its own way. Keita proclaimed his nation the Republic of Mali and tentatively linked up with the Ghana-Guinea Union in July 1961. The addition of Mali did little to eliminate the Union's original difficulties. In 1963, the personal rivalry between Touré and Nkrumah, fueled by Ghana's alleged implication in the assassination of Togo's president, Sylvanus Olympio, hastened the demise of the Ghana-Guinea-Mali Union.

With the notable exception of Guinea and Mali, the French-speaking West African states during this period concentrated on alliances, such as the Council of the Entente, created in May 1959, the basis of which was mutual economic assistance. The Council was Félix Houphouët-Boigny's brainchild. It was expected that the nearly destitute members, Upper Volta and Niger, would provide workers for the plantations of the Ivory Coast and the ports of Dahomey. To be sure, there were policy disagreements and even open hostility among the Council nations. But also present was a spirit of cooperation and a mature perspective on what an underdeveloped nation's priorities should be. While Kwame Nkrumah and his followers were obsessed with Africa's political future, the other French and English-speaking West African leaders, while supporting Pan-Africanism's precepts, were more concerned with the future of their own nations. So it was that by 1960 two West African political camps—one militant, the other moderate—were distinguishable.

In the summer of 1960 the Congo exploded. In December the French-speaking nations gathered at Brazzaville, ostensibly to seek a way to restore peace in the Congo. Moderation and reason set the tone of the meeting as they did in May 1961 when the Brazzaville states — which had come to be known as the Union Africain et Malagache (UAM) — reconvened in Monrovia, Liberia.

As a counterforce to the UAM (which Nkrumah considered a threat to his quest for Pan-African leadership and political domination) another conference, this time at Casablanca, was called to order in January 1961. Ghana, Guinea, Mali, Morocco, the United Arab Republic, Libya, and Ceylon sent delegates. The rhetoric was familiar. Nkrumah accused the West (with some justification, for many European and American corporations had invested heavily in the Congo's valuable mineral resources) of interference in the Congo on the side of what he termed reactionary, neo-colonial forces. He called for the support of the Lumumbists, followers of Patrice Lumumba, the Congo's deposed premier, who died under mysterious circumstances in February 1961. The UAM, on the other hand, backed the government of the Congo's president, Joseph Kasavubu.

Relations between the moderate UAM and the militant Casablanca nations continued to worsen, especially after Sylvanus Olympio's murder in January 1963. The dark suspicions of Ghanaian involvement that surrounded the act sent shock waves throughout Africa. Fortunately, its leaders recognized the pitfalls of polarization. Rather than permit inter-African quarrels to continue unchecked, a major effort toward reconciliation was undertaken.

In May 1963, thirty-two nations sent delegates representing more than 200 million Africans to a conference at Addis Ababa, Ethiopia. Though the debates were often vitriolic and differences between nations barely concealed, remarkable statesmanship, compromise, and conciliation carried the day. On May 25 the Organization of African Unity, a mini-United Nations, was chartered. Its appearance was followed by the disbanding of the Casablanca group, and the UAM later evolved into an almost purely economic alliance, the Organisation Commune Africain et Malagache (OCAM).

The OAU has been severely tried and tested in the few years since its birth. Like the United Nations, its record of achievement is mixed. It has settled a number of nagging border questions, but a solution to Africa's most traumatic conflict — the Biafran war — continually eluded it. Yet the OAU at least provides a framework, imperfect though it may be, within which inter-African disputes can be subjected to rational discussion and counsel before they reach the flashpoint of bloodshed.

The brief national profiles that follow trace the checkered progress of West Africa's new states (except for Sierra Leone and Liberia which were discussed earlier), during the 1960s and consider the immediate and future prospects of each nation.

Gambia

As early as the fifteenth century, Portuguese mariners ventured ashore in the swampy land later to be known as Gambia. Most of the seagoing European nations traded with Gambia's coastal tribes until the country was annexed by Great Britain after the Treaty of Versailles (1783). Gambia became a British Crown Colony in 1843, remaining a part of Great Britain's West African empire until she gained her independence in 1965.

Gambia, surrounded by Senegal, is a prime example of mindless imperial "nation-making." Because of their peculiar geographic position and homogeneous populations a number of hitherto unsuccessful efforts have been made to integrate the two nations. Only 29,000 of Gambia's 325,000 citizens live in Bathurst, her capital and Atlantic port city The major tribal affiliations in this overwhelmingly Muslim nation are the Mandingo, Fula, and Wolof peoples

Gambia's prime minister is Sir Dawda Kairaba Jawara, the leader of the Progressive People's Party. The political opposition in one of the West Africa's few remaining multi-party states is provided by Pierre Sar N'Jie's United Party, and the Democratic Congress Alliance (DCA).

Gambia's natural resources are limited and groundnuts comprise nearly ninety-five percent of her exports. With her future survival dependent upon massive foreign aid and technical assistance, Gambia's economic prospects in the years to come are less than encouraging.

Ghana

Ghana is situated a few degrees above the Equator

on the Gulf of Guinea. To the north lies Upper
Volta, to the west the Ivory Coast, and to the east
the Republic of Togo. Ghana's seat of government
is Accra, a bustling, modern city of 500,000. The
Ashanti spiritual and cultural center, Kumasi, has
250,000 inhabitants. More than fifty dialects and
languages are spoken by the many ethnic groups
which make up Ghana's 8.6 million population. The
largest of these are the Akan and Fanti of the coast,
the Guans of the Volta River region, the Ashanti in
the forest area to the north, the Ga and Ewe in what
was formerly British Togoland, and the Mossi-Da-
gomba tribes living in the Northern Territories.

Shortly after independence in 1957, the Convention Peoples' Party superseded the government as
Kwame Nkrumah began to arrogate more and more
power to himself. In his pursuit of a united, strongly
centralized Africa, he managed to alienate a number
of African leaders as well as many of the former
colonial nations which disapproved of his overtures
to the Communist bloc.

Internally, Ghana was struck in 1961 by serious
labor disturbances. A general strike was suppressed
by government forces and, in the aftermath, Nkrumah had his political mentor, Dr. Joseph Danquah,
arrested and tried for treason. Dr. Danquah died in
prison four years later. Two assassination attempts,
one in 1962 and another in 1964, resulted in intensified government repression. Nkrumah isolated
himself and declared Ghana a one-party state. By
this time, however, his popularity had eroded enor-

mously. It came as no surprise when, in February 1966, while en route to Peking, he was deposed by the Ghanaian army. On his return from China, Nkrumah patched up his quarrel with Sékou Touré and took refuge in Guinea where, in March, he was given the honorary title of Joint Head of State.

In Accra, his cabinet was dismissed, the CPP and the National Assembly were dissolved, and the constitution suspended. A National Liberation Council, directed by General Joseph Ankrah, replaced the government and ruled until elections were held in August 1969. When the votes were tallied, it was shown that Dr. Kofi A. Busia's Progress Party had garnered a majority of the seats in the reconstituted National Assembly. A new government was installed in October 1969 with Dr Busia, an Ashanti, as premier In August 1970, Edward Akufo-Addo was elected Ghana's president. For the first time in a decade, an opposition group, the Justice Party of Nkrumah's finance minister, K. A. Gbedemah, was allowed to exist.

The promise of Ghana's resilient economy has not been realized, mainly because of mismanagement during Nkrumah's regime. In all fairness, it must be said that his administration did provide a basis for much of Ghana's industrial growth. Nkrumah, for example, encouraged the construction of the Akosombo hydroelectric plant in order to harness the power of the Volta River. Although Ghana is rich in mineral resources, produces one-third of the world's cocoa, and exports substantial amounts of coffee and palm products, she is laboring under a punishing national debt, a carryover from Nkrumah's time in office. Fortunately, headway in rescheduling payment of these obligations is being made and Ghana is slowly returning to economic normalcy.

Nigeria

Nigeria is a sprawling land of swamps, lagoons, rain forests, plateaus, desert, and large, navigable rivers which flow into the Gulf of Guinea.

With 54 million people she is Africa's most populous nation. Over 250 tribal groups, the largest of which are the Hausa-Fulani, the Yoruba, and the Ibo, make up her heterogeneous population. Nigeria is a nation marked by strong regional ties and brutal inter-tribal rivalries. The Hausa-Fulani, Nupe, Tiv, and Kanuri predominate in the Muslim North; the Yorubas, Binis, and Ijaws dwell in the West and Midwest regions. The East is the home of the Ibos, Efiks, and Ibibios.

From its beginnings Nigeria has been a starcrossed, highly politicized nation. It came into being through compromise when its major political parties, which reflected Nigeria's regional and religious biases, temporarily set aside their differences. Almost simultaneously, the ever-present regional tensions burst forth. The arrest and imprisonment of Chief Obafemi Awolowo by Chief Samuel Akintola, and Akintola's subsequent manipulation of the regional elections, further aggravated an already rapidly deteriorating situation. By late 1965, Nigeria was sharply split between two political factions—the Nigerian National Alliance in the North and the Eastern or Ibo-dominated United Progressive Grand Alliance. The UPGA boycotted the election while the Northern Region's premier, Sir Ahmadu Bello, aligned himself with Akintola.

Nigeria's political stability had been badly shaken by Akintola's brazen performance. Governmental corruption had become commonplace. The Ibos, in particular, were thoroughly alienated and resentful. On the night of January 15, 1966, disgruntled Ibo officers took matters into their own hands and shot Sir Ahmadu Bello. Akintola and Nigeria's federal Prime Minister, Sir Abubakar Tafawa Balewa, suffered the same fate. Their bodies were discovered near the national capital of Lagos. In that one night of terrible violence, Nigeria had lost three of its national leaders and a number of Muslim officers. Soon after these assassinations an Ibo general, J. T. U. Aguiyi-Ironsi, took command of the government.

Ironsi's rule was cut short on July 29, 1966 when he was murdered during a mutiny of Northern army officers. General Yakubu Gowon, a Northern Christian, replaced Ironsi as Supreme Military Commander of the new Federal Military Government.

Unfortunately, Nigeria's troubles had just begun. In May, the Northern Region's cities were the scene of massacres as Ibos fled eastward to escape the vengeance of Hausa mobs. Despite efforts to bring the two camps to the conference table, the killing of Ibos continued. When 30,000 Ibos lost their lives at the hands of avenging Muslims in May and September 1966, the breach between Ibo and Hausa became irreparable. Finally, on May 30, 1967 Colonel C. Odumegwu Ojukwu, as military governor of the Eastern Region, severed relations with Lagos and proclaimed the independence of the Republic of Biafra. As we have seen, the bloodshed, terror, and destruction that followed did not end until Biafra, badly beaten, surrendered on January 15, 1970.

Fortunately, Nigeria is blessed with a wealth of natural resources (mineral deposits, including oil, iron, cocoa, groundnuts, palm products, and rubber), an effective communications system, and more miles of railroad track than any other West African nation. The oil-rich Eastern Region, its industrial facilities incapacitated during the civil war, is now on the slow road to recovery.

For Nigeria to survive as a nation the psychological wounds of war must be healed. General Gowon's military government has adopted (officially, at least), a policy of reintegrating the Biafrans into Nigerian society. Whether the long-standing hatreds that plague Nigeria can be erased by governmental efforts at reconciliation is doubtful. Nigeria's future, however, hinges upon the government's success in at least reducing the intensity of these antagonisms.

Cameroon

The Federal Republic of Cameroon is often referred to as the "hinge" of Africa. It lies on the Gulf of Guinea east and south of Nigeria and is composed of two states: East Cameroon (formerly the Republic of Cameroun) and West Cameroon (originally the southern sector of the British Cameroons). Her capital is Yaoundé, but the port of Douala, with a population of 230,000, is her largest city.

Cameroon is one of the most ethnically diverse nations in West Africa. Over 140 tribes live in this nation of rain forests, plateaus, mountains, and marshland. More than half of Cameroon's 4.8 million people still adhere to their traditional religions. The remainder are either Muslim (North) or Christian (South).

When Cameroon became independent in 1961, the Union Cameroonaise (UC) of Ahmadou Ahidjo, came to power. Ahidjo, the son of a Fulani chief, sought to consolidate his power and, in 1966, the opposition Kamerun National Democratic Party (KNDP) was dissolved. Each of Cameroon's political parties was absorbed into a single, all-inclusive party, the Union National Cameroonaise (UNC).

Cameroon's economy is based on agriculture. She exports coffee, cocoa, cotton, bananas, and palm products, primarily to the Common Market countries of Western Europe. French corporations are financing the mining of Cameroon's extensive bauxite deposits. Because of the combination of rapid economic advancement and industrial expansion, Cameroon's future is one of the most promising in West Africa.

Dahomey

Dahomey is a country smaller in area than Pennsylvania. It is bordered by Nigeria and the Niger
Basin on the east, on the west by Togo, on the
northwest by Upper Volta, on the north by Niger,
and on the south by the Gulf of Guinea. Dahomey's
capital is Porto Novo, a former slave outlet, though
most of the government's functions are performed
in Cotonou. Its coastline is riddled with lagoons,
while the hinterland is marked by both swampland
and dense vegetation. To the northwest lie the Ata-
cora Mountains. At least forty-two different tribal
groupings, among them the Fons, Yoruba, Adjas,
and the Baribas, are represented in Dahomey's 2.6
million population.

The 1960s were a decade of violence for Dahomey. The political seesaw began in October 1963
when the civilian government of President Hubert
Maga was overthrown by Colonel Christophe Soglo.
In the 1964 general elections Sourou-Migan Apithy
was chosen president. By November 1965, however,
the Apithy regime's repeated internal crises and
wasteful spending led to another Soglo-staged coup.
This time, the colonel retained power until he, too,
was removed from office by the military in December
1967. The revolt's leader, Colonel Alphonse Alley,
assumed the presidency, promising a swift return
to civilian rule.

The military government drew up a new constitution and scheduled elections for May 1968. Apithy,
in exile, urged a boycott of the polls. Alley, in re-

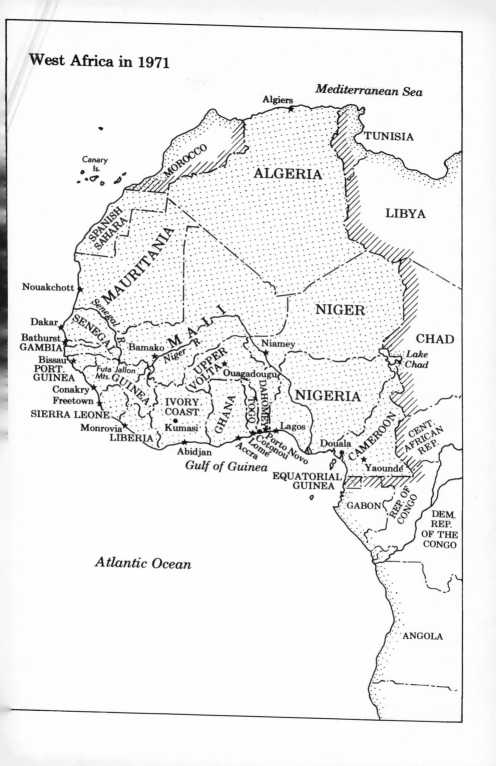

West Africa in 1971

sponse, invalidated the election results. Subsequently, Dr. Émile-Derlin Zinsou was authorized to form a government. In December 1969, Zinsou ran afoul of the army and was deposed. A military triumvirate replaced him and soon after permitted the return from exile of Dahomey's former presidents, Maga and Apithy. Hubert Maga, in office when the cycle of coups first began, became head of the Government of National Unity in May 1970.

Even by West African standards Dahomey has a relatively low per capita income which reflects her underdeveloped agricultural economy. Palm products, coffee, groundnuts, and cotton are her major cash crops and industrialization is still in a nascent state. Recent exploratory drilling, however, has indicated the presence of oil deposits. If these are promising enough to develop, they could revolutionize Dahomey's currently lack-lustre economy.

Guinea

Guinea, a land the size of Oregon, lies on the "bulge" of West Africa. To its north are Portuguese Guinea and Senegal, to the northeast Mali, and to the southeast the Ivory Coast. Its southern border is shared with Sierra Leone and Liberia. Guinea's narrow coastal belt rises gradually to the Futa Jallon highlands where the rivers Niger, Gambia, and Senegal have their headwaters.

Nearly 113,000 of the 3.7 million Guineans live in the capital city of Conakry. The most populous of her more than sixteen ethnic groups are the Fulani, the Mandingos, and the Susu. Most of Guinea's people practice the Islamic faith.

Guinea's president is Sékou Touré, a leader who has brought his nation through a number of crises. In September 1958, when Guinea proudly rejected membership in the French Community and opted for independence, France retaliated by withdrawing all technical and economic aid. The other Western nations were slow to respond with assistance and Touré, his alternatives limited, turned for help to the Soviet Union. Despite his cordial relations with the Soviet bloc, Touré has managed to remain unaligned, choosing instead to follow his own star. During the past decade Guinea's relations with France, the United States, Great Britain, the Ivory Coast, and Ghana have been strained periodically, yet Touré has succeeded, in each case, in mending his political fences. His break with Kwame Nkrumah over the assassination of Sylvanus Olympio has been repaired and, as noted earlier, Ghana's deposed premier has enjoyed political asylum in Guinea since 1966.

Sékou Touré's undisguised sympathy with and active support of the rebels of Portuguese Guinea— Amilcar Cabral's PAIGC operates from bases in Guinea—inspired the November 1970 assault by Portuguese-supported mercenaries. (See section on Portuguese Guinea, page 225.)

Guinea's Soviet-equipped army ultimately turned back the invading forces after they had razed a number of buildings in Conakry.

While long strides have been made in both industry and agriculture, many of Guinea's people still eke out a living on her banana plantations. Guinea, however, has one-third of the world's high-grade bauxite reserves. If these are developed, along with her diamond, gold, and iron deposits, Guinea's great economic potential should eventually be realized.

Ivory Coast

The Ivory Coast is the richest and most self-sufficient of France's former West African colonies. Slightly larger than New Mexico, its Atlantic coastline is split with lagoons, in the center of which is Abidjan, the Ivory Coast's capital and deep-water port. Behind the coast lie lush tropical forests and plains. In the northwest are the Man Mountains. Over sixty tribes combine to make up the Ivory Coast's five million people, the largest of which are the Akan, the Kru, and the Mane. One-quarter of her population is Muslim.

The man most responsible for the Ivory Coast's comparative political stability is Félix Houphouët-Boigny, the founder of the RDA and later the Council of the Entente, and the head of his nation's only political party, the Parti Démocratique de la Côte d'Ivoire (PDCI). During Houphouët's regime, coffee (the Ivory Coast is the world's third largest producer), cocoa, and banana crops have been successfully grown and exported; diamonds and manganese have been mined in substantial quantities. Her agricultural diversification and industrial expansion have kept the Ivory Coast on an even economic keel.

Houphouët's rule has not been entirely free of challenge. In 1963, a plot against him was foiled and in 1968 a demonstration in support of breakaway Biafra ended in rioting and looting. The Ivory Coast ultimately became the only West African state to officially recognize Biafra. In May 1968, students, in sympathy with their French counterparts, fought with Ivoirian police in the streets of Abidjan. Since 1968, however, the Ivory Coast has been quiet and has steadily pursued a policy of Eurafrican economic cooperation.

Mali

Mali, like Upper Volta and Niger, has the dubious distinction of lacking direct access to the sea. Its enormous land mass, three times the size of California, ranges in terrain from desert to savannah and forest. The Niger River, its only route to the Gulf of Guinea, is navigable only half the year. Most of Mali's five million people are farmers, fishermen, and cattle herders. The Bambara, Malinke, and Sarakole tribesmen are in the majority, although there is also a large Fulani and Songhai population. Until recently, the nomadic Taureg, the fierce warriors of ancient times, presented a problem for the central government whose authority they refused to recognize.

Modern Mali was within Samori's sphere before his capture by the French in 1898. Centuries before, it had been part of the empires of Sundiata, Askia Muhammad, and Sunni Ali. Mali's heritage is a glorious one, and one can understand why she regards herself as the spiritual heir of the pre-colonial African empires.

With Senegal, Mali (then known as the French Soudan), voted for autonomy within the French Community in 1959 as the Mali Federation. With Léopold Senghor as its president and Mali's Modibo Keita as prime minister, this association was troubled from its very beginnings. Keita, like Kwame Nkrumah, favored a strongly centralized government, a concept vigorously opposed by Senghor. Matters worsened, states of emergency were declared, the pro-Senegalese army rebelled, and Keita was arrested. In August 1960 Senegal seceded and the Mali Federation collapsed. Keita, in turn, removed himself to his capital of Bamako and soon after proclaimed Soudan the Republic of Mali. For a brief period, Mali joined the Ghana-Guinea Union but this arrangement was dissolved by 1963.

Modibo Keita served Mali as its president from 1960 until November 1968. In January of that year the National Assembly was abolished. This act, coupled with Mali's economic tailspin, precipitated a coup. The dissidents' leader, Captain Yoro Diakité, replaced the presidency with the Comité-Militaire de Libération Nationale (CMLN) which still governs Mali.

Mali is an impoverished nation. Its main crops are millet, rice, and cotton. While French technicians have experienced some success in growing cotton, livestock remains Mali's most important resource. Deposits of bauxite, uranium, and phosphates have been located but as yet they have not been mined. Progress in agricultural development, though hampered by a lack of modern technology, is one of the few bright spots in Mali's immediate future.

Mauritania

Mauritania, the last of France's West African colonies to gain her independence, is as large as Texas and California combined. A desolate land, she was referred to as "the void" by the French soldiers and officials stationed there. Most of the 1.2 million people who inhabit this hot and arid Sahara country trace their origin to the Berber tribes who migrated southward during the eleventh century. Many are nomads who roam the desert and live an existence similar to that of their ancestors. Twenty-five thousand Mauritanians live in her recently constructed Atlantic Coast capital of Nouakchott.

This Islamic republic is ruled by the Mauritanian People's Party (Hizb es Sha'b). Mauritania's president, Moktar Ould Daddah, re-elected in 1966, has attempted to secure his own position by outlawing rival political parties. Except for Morocco's long-standing claim to sovereignty over Mauritania—a position Morocco abandoned in 1969—the nation has suffered few threats to her stability. The equilibrium was upset once in 1966 when black African and Moorish students fought one another in Nouakchott and again in 1968 when students rioted in sympathy with the French student revolt.

Mauritania's economy is based on palms, fishing,

and livestock. However, the mining of copper and iron deposits, with European technical assistance, is favorably changing Mauritania's economic picture.

Niger

Like Mauritania, Niger is mostly desert, and arable land in this isolated nation is at a premium. Enclosed by Algeria, Libya, Chad, Dahomey, Upper Volta, and Mali, Niger has changed little since the explorers Mungo Park and Heinrich Barth trekked across her vast expanse in the nineteenth century. Her 3.7 million people, the majority of whom are Hausa, Djerma-Songhai, Fulani, Kanuri, and Taureg tribesmen, survive by raising cattle in this country which has no rail transportation.

President Diori Hamani has ruled Niger from the capital of Niamey since 1960. Diori's reign has not been uneventful, his most strenuous opposition coming from his exiled rival, Djibo Bakary, whose followers have made frequent forays across Niger's borders. Diori managed to crush an army mutiny in 1963 and, in 1965, an assassination attempt was thwarted. Diori's party, the Parti Progréssiste Nigerien (PPN), an offshoot of the old RDA, is Niger's only legal political group.

While the groundnut remains Niger's major export, the discovery of uranium, iron, tin, and copper deposits, French financial assistance, and a growing economic relationship with her wealthier neighbor Nigeria all lend support to the belief that Niger's economy will improve significantly during the next decade.

Upper Volta

Upper Volta is a landlocked nation, slightly larger than Colorado, and ranging in topography from swampland to desert and plateau. Her capital and major city, Ougadougou, shelters 100,000 of Upper Volta's 5 million people. Upper Volta is the ancestral home of the Mossi who successfully resisted both European and Muslim penetration until late in the nineteenth century. Islam, in fact, has made few inroads among the Mossi farmers and the traditional Mossi king, the *morho-noba*, still wields a great deal of political power.

Riots and labor unrest inspired by corruption and rampant inflation in this severely impoverished land brought down the regime of Upper Volta's first president, Maurice Yaméogo, in January 1966. The political vacuum created by Yaméogo's overthrow was quickly filled by Lieutenant-Colonel (now General) Sangoule Lamizana. Lamizana suspended the 1960 constitution and has ruled since his takeover at the head of a civilian-military government.

Upper Volta's lifeline is her rail link — built with Mossi labor — to the Ivory Coast's port capital of Abidjan, over which her meager agricultural exports are carried. With foreign aid and technical assistance, progress has been made in streamlining and improving Upper Volta's subsistence economy. She remains, however, among the poorest of West Africa's nations.

Senegal

Senegal's landscape is dotted with plains, savannahs, foothills, and the Futa Jallon mountains. It is also drained by four large rivers — the Senegal, Gambia, Saloum, and Casamance — each of which is navigable for some distance inland by ocean-going ships. It is approximately the size of South Dakota, surrounds tiny Gambia, and is bordered by Mauritania, Mali, Guinea, and Portuguese Guinea. The Wolof, Fulani, Serer, and Mandingo peoples are Senegal's major tribes and eighty percent of Senegal's population of four million is Muslim. Large numbers of Europeans and Syrians live in Dakar, the national capital, and the port of Saint Louis.

After his contretemps with Modibo Keita and the dissolution of the Federation of Mali, Léopold Senghor, Senegal's poet-president, faced yet another threat. In December 1962, an attempted coup by his Prime Minister, Mamadou Dia, was aborted and Senghor, in retaliation, had the post of prime minister abolished. In 1966, Senghor's Union Progréssiste Sénégalaise (UPS) became Senegal's only lawful political party. In 1968, after Senghor was re-elected president by an overwhelming majority, Dakar was struck by a two-fold rebellion. Students at the University of Dakar, emboldened by the May revolt in France, took to the streets. This outbreak, matched by peasant demonstrations over a decline in the price of groundnuts, raged for some time before order was restored. In 1969, student unrest flared once more in the face of increasing governmental restrictions.

Senegal, more than her sister nations, has an adequate system of communications, installed by France with whom she shared a special colonial relationship. While she is still heavily dependent upon her groundnut crop, Senegal's economy, through state planning, is being diversified. With Mali, Guinea, and Mauritania, she organized the Senegal River States Organization (D.E.R.S.) in order to develop the river basin through hydroelectric plants and dams. Though her importance in West Africa has declined since the days when Dakar—the "Paris of Africa"—was France's West African administrative center, and her economy has temporarily stagnated, Senegal has taken measures to improve her shaky economic position.

Togo

Togo's one and a half million people were granted their independence in 1960, when the nation's head was Sylvanus Olympio, one of Africa's most respected statesmen. Olympio sought to unify the Ewe peoples scattered by the colonial mapmakers between Togo and her western neighbor, the Republic of Ghana, which had inherited British Togoland following a 1956 referendum. Kwame Nkrumah had no intention of accommodating the Togolese president. Olympio, in turn, described Nkrumah as a "black imperialist" and tensions between the two increased.

Olympio's anti-military philosophy and the declining economic fortunes of his nation weakened his domestic position. On January 13, 1963, Sylvanus Olympio was assassinated in Lomé, Togo's capital city, and West Africa lost one of its most promising and able leaders. At first Ghana was suspected of complicity in Olympio's murder, Nkrumah was denounced, and many African nations withheld recognition of the successor government of Nicolas Grunitzky, Olympio's brother-in-law.

Grunitzky, however, proved to be a moderate, low-keyed leader who never quite achieved broad-based public support. In November 1966, Olympio's former supporters demonstrated over the nation's deteriorating economy. In January 1967, the embattled Grunitzky government was forced to resign. General Étienne Eyadema, a military strongman who later admitted firing the fatal shots that felled Olympio, seized power and, in 1968, declared himself president.

Unlike his predecessors, Eyadema has become an increasingly popular figure among the Togolese. The nation's economy has been stabilized and Togo's lucrative coffee and cocoa exports have enabled her to balance her budget without French aid. Development of her phosphate resources has further improved her trading position. While Togo's people have begun to benefit from these advances, economic prosperity remains a distant, though attainable, goal.

Portuguese Guinea

Portuguese Guinea is Portugal's last outpost in West Africa. In 1446, the Portuguese captain Nuno Tristão anchored off this poor land of swamps, rivers, and steaming forests. In the centuries that followed, both France and Great Britain repeatedly contested Portugal's territorial claim. In 1870, with President Ulysses S. Grant acting as mediator, Portugal's "right of cession" was recognized and the thin slice of West African land was attached to her overseas empire.

Portuguese Guinea is bordered by Guinea and Senegal. To the west lies the Atlantic Ocean on which Bissau, her capital, is situated. Her most populous tribes are the Balante, Fula, Madyako, and Mende. Muslims number less than 200,000 and there are fewer than 25,000 Christians in her population of something between 600,000 and 800,000.

The explosive atmosphere in Portugal's Overseas Provinces or territories—Angola, Mozambique, and Portuguese Guinea—makes it necessary for her to maintain a force of more than 100,000 troops in Africa. This places a severe burden on Portugal's own unhealthy economy. The internal affairs of her colonies are controlled by Lisbon, but Portugal has recently indicated its willingness to give these possessions more local autonomy.

Portuguese Guinea has a long, unhappy history of violence and strife. In 1931, a nationalist rebellion occurred. On August 3, 1959 a strike by Bissau dockworkers ended in the killing of a number of strikers. As a result of these executions, the numerous clandestine independence movements began to gain adherents. The most active and effective of these groups is the African Independence Party of Guinea and Cape Verde Islands (PAIGC), led by the British-educated agronomist, Amilcar Cabral. Its headquarters are in Conakry, Guinea—one of the prime military objectives of the November 1970 Portuguese-equipped invasion—from which it conducts raids across Portuguese Guinea's borders. It is estimated that at least two-thirds of Portuguese Guinea is under the nationalists' control. At this rate, the last bastion of European colonialism in West Africa should fall before the middle of the seventies.

What lies ahead for a West Africa whose future is inextricably entwined with the future of the world? The political pressures, which occasionally drew West Africa into the vortex of the Cold War in the sixties, have not disappeared. Nor has the dangerous temptation to take advantage of the global competition among the superpowers. More and more, however, West Africa's leaders have come to realize that political nonalignment, rather than brinkmanship, is the most fruitful path to follow.

Although the nagging problems that retard much

of West Africa's economic growth remain, the "one crop" economy—colonialism's most enduring economic legacy—is slowly being abandoned in favor of industrial and agricultural diversification. International technical assistance is still insufficient to enable her to cope with the needs and rising costs of industrialization, health care, and education, but state planning and regional cooperation are helping many of West Africa's nations to overcome the obstacles to prosperity.

Another ever-present threat to the achievement of social and political stability is tribalism. Few West African states have anything like homogeneous populations. All are cursed with artificial borders. The people cast together within these nations often do not share a common language, heritage, or means of livelihood. Deadly rivalries arising from such differences exist between ethnic groups in many of the world's countries. West Africa is no exception. In order to eliminate this problem, each of West Africa's governments is striving to create a strong national identity, one which transcends tribal affiliations and biases, and instills in each citizen a sense of unity and community.

With good cause it has often been said that those who fail to learn from history are forced to relive it. History provides us with many tragic examples. Of course, any nation's survival may often depend upon circumstances beyond its control—its ethnic composition, its wealth or lack of natural resources, or even its geographical position. It can also rest upon the policies and judgment of its leaders. West Africa's leaders clearly recognize that the errors in judgment and planning which led to economic fiasco in Ghana, or the arrogation of power which resulted in military coups in Mali and Dahomey, or the unchecked tribal hostilities which culminated in the Nigerian civil war, must not be repeated. These statemen are committed to the prevention of a repetition of these and other events which combined to mar West Africa's first decade of independence. It is with this optimistic commitment that the nations of West Africa are being launched into the seventies.

THE TRIBES OF WEST AFRICA

Tribes	*Nations*
Adja	Dahomey
Adja-Watyi	Togo
Agni-Baule	Ivory Coast
Ashanti	Ghana, Ivory Coast
Ahanta	Ghana
Aizo	Dahomey
Baga	Guinea
Balante	Portuguese Guinea
Bambara (Mandingo)	Gambia, Guinea, Ivory Coast, Liberia, Mali, Senegal, Sierra Leone
Bariba	Dahomey
Bete (Kru)	Guinea, Ivory Coast, Liberia
Beriberi	Niger
Bobo	Mali, Upper Volta
Dan	Ivory Coast
Dendi	Dahomey
Diola	Senegal, Upper Volta
Djerma-Songhai	Niger
Dogon	Mali
Efiks	Nigeria
Evalue	Ghana
Ewe	Ghana, Togo
Fang	Cameroon
Fanti	Ghana, Liberia
Fon	Dahomey
Fula	Gambia, Portuguese Guinea
Fulani	Cameroon, Dahomey, Guinea, Nigeria, Senegal, Sierra Leone, Upper Volta
Gojas	Liberia
Gonja	Ghana
Hausa	Niger, Nigeria, Upper Volta
Holli	Dahomey
Ibibio	Nigeria

Tribes	*Nations*
Ibo	Nigeria
Ijaw	Nigeria
Jolah	Gambia
Kabrai-Losso	Togo
Kanuri	Niger, Nigeria
Kissi	Guinea, Sierra Leone
Kono	Guinea, Sierra Leone
Kpelle	Liberia
Krim	Sierra Leone
Kuniagi	Guinea
Kwa Kwa	Ivory Coast
Landoumas	Guinea, Sierra Leone
Lebu	Senegal
Lobi	Upper Volta
Madyako	Portuguese Guinea
Manons	Guinea
Mende	Sierra Leone, Portuguese Guinea
Moors	Mali
Moshi-Dagomba	Ghana, Upper Volta
Mossi	Mali, Upper Volta
Nalous	Guinea
Nzima	Ghana
Peulhs	Guinea, Mali, Niger, Senegal
Pilapila	Dahomey
Senufo	Ivory Coast, Mali, Upper Volta
Serer	Senegal
Sombas	Dahomey
Sonraig	Mali
Susu	Guinea
Taureg	Mali, Niger, Upper Volta
Temne	Sierra Leone
Tukolor	Senegal
Twi	Ghana, Togo
Vai	Liberia, Sierra Leone
Wolof	Gambia, Senegal
Yoruba	Dahomey, Nigeria

NOTES

1. Quoted in H. R. Palmer, *Sudanese Memoirs* (Lagos, 1928), Vol. 2.
2. Quoted in Margaret Shinnie, *Ancient African Kingdoms* (London, 1965).
3. Ibn Hawqal (Baron de Slane, transl.), *Description de l'-Afrique* (Paris, 1842).
4. Al-Bakri (W. MacGuckin and Baron de Slane, transl.), *Description de l'Afrique septentrionale* (Algiers, 1913).
5. Mahmout Kati (O. Houdas and M. Delafosse, transl.), *Tarikh al-Fattash* (Paris, 1913).
6. Quoted in Shinnie, *op. cit.*
7. Quoted in Maurice Delafosse, *Traditions historiques et lengendaires du Soudan occidental* (Paris, 1913).
8. H. A. R. Gibb, *Ibn Battuta, Travels in Asia and Africa* (London, 1929).
9. Leo Africanus, *The History and Description of Africa done into English by John Pory*, ed. Robert Brown (London, 1896).
10. Maurice Delafosse (F. Fligelman, transl.), *The Negroes of Africa: History and Culture* (Washington, 1931). Reprinted 1968.
11. Leo Africanus, *op. cit.*
12. *Ibid.*
13. Quoted in Palmer, *op. cit.*
14. Yakut (F. Wustenfeld, transl.), *Mu'jam al-Buldan.* 6 vols. (Leipzig, 1886–73).
15. Ibn Khaldun (Baron de Slane, transl.), *Histoire des Berberes et des Dynasties Musulmanes de l'Afrique septentrionale* (Paris, 1925).
16. Leo Africanus, *op. cit.*
17. *Ibid.*
18. Quoted in Palmer, *op. cit.*

19. Hugh Clapperton, Dixon Denham, and Walter Oudney, *Narrative of Travels and Discoveries in Northern and Central Africa in the years 1822, 1823, and 1824* (London, 1826).

20. Delafosse, *The Negroes of Africa, op. cit.*

21. Heinrich Barth, *Travels and Discoveries in North and Central Africa* (London, 1857).

22. Quoted in Palmer, *op. cit..*

23. Leo Africanus, *op. cit.*

24. Quoted in Palmer, *op. cit.*

25. Barth, *op. cit.*

26. Quoted in E. J. Arnett, *The Rise of the Sokoto Fulani* (Kano, 1929).

27. Leo Africanus, *op. cit.*

28. Barth, *op. cit.*

29. Quoted in Arnett, *op. cit.*

30. Samuel Johnson, *History of the Yorubas* (London, 1921).

31. Quoted in T. Hodgkin, *Nigerian Perspectives* (London, 1960).

32. Quoted in Richard Hakluyt, *The Principal Navigations, Voyages, Traffiques, & Discoveries of the English Nation* (Glasgow, 1903–05). Reprinted 1965.

33. Quoted in Hodgkin, *op. cit.*

34. Quoted in Hakluyt, *op. cit.*

35. Quoted in J. W. Blake, *Europeans in West Africa, 1450–1560*, 2 vols (London, 1942).

36. Quoted in Hakluyt, *op. cit.*

37. T. E. Bowdich, *Mission from Cape Castle to Ashantee* (London, 1819).

38. Archibald Dalzell, *History of Dahomey, An Inland Kingdom of Africa* (London, 1793).

39. Robert Norris, *Memoirs of the Reign of Bossa Ahadee* [Tegbesu], *King of Dahomy* (London, 1789).

40. Sir Richard Burton, *A Mission to Gelele, King of Dahome* (London, 1864). Reprinted 1966.

41. Quoted in Arnett, *op. cit.*

42. Quoted in Clapperton, Denham, and Oudney, *op. cit.*

43. W. Winwood Reade, *Savage Africa* (London, 1863).

44. *Ibid.*

45. Captain John Adams, *Remarks on the Country extending from Cape Palmas to the River Kongo* (London, 1823).

46. Quoted in Jean Trepp, "The Liverpool Movement for the Abolition of the English Slave Trade," *Journal of Negro History*, XIII (July, 1928).

47. Quoted in Blake, *op. cit.*

48. Quoted in Trepp, *op. cit.*

49. Quoted in H. C. Luke, *A Bibliography of Sierra Leone* (London, 1925). Reprinted 1969.

50. Quoted in Hakluyt, *op. cit.*

51. William Lloyd Garrison, *Thoughts on African Colonization* (Boston, 1832). Reprinted 1968.

52. *Ibid.*

53. Brantz Mayer, *Captain Canot; or Twenty Years of an African Slaver* (New York, 1854). Reprinted 1968.

54. John Gunther, *Inside Africa* (New York, 1955).

55. E. Hertslet, *Map of Africa by Treaty*, 3 vols. (London, 1894).

56. Gunther, *op. cit.*

57. Mungo Park, *Travels in the Interior Districts of Africa, 1795, 1796, and 1797.* 5th ed. (London, 1807). Reprinted 1970.

58. Amy Jacques Garvey, *The Philosophy and Opinions of Marcus Garvey* (New York, 1923). Reprinted 1968.

59. George Padmore, *How Britain Rules Africa* (London, 1936). Reprinted 1969.

60. Martin R. Delany, *The Condition, Elevation, Emigration and Destiny of the Colored People of the United States* (Philadelphia, 1852).

61. C. Odumegwu Ojukwu, *Biafra*, 2 vols. (New York, 1969).

62. *The New York Times*, January 14, 1970.

63. *Ibid.*

64. Obafemi Awolowo, *Path to Nigerian Freedom* (London, 1947).

65. James Africanus B. Horton, *West African Countries and Peoples* (London, 1868). Reprinted 1969.

66. Kwame Nkrumah, *I Speak of Freedom* (London, 1961).

A SELECTED BIBLIOGRAPHY

In addition to those works cited in the Notes, the following books are highly recommended for further reading. Titles marked with an asterisk are available in a paperbound edition.

A. Primary Sources and General Works

*Abraham, W. E. *The Mind Of Africa.* Chicago, 1962.

*Bohannan, Paul. *Africa and the Africans.* New York, 1964.

*Davidson, Basil. *The African Past.* Boston, 1964.

*————. *A History of West Africa to the Nineteenth Century.* New York, 1966.

*DuBois, W. E. B. *The World and Africa.* New York, 1947.

*Fage, John D. *An Introduction to the History of West Africa.* 5th ed. Cambridge, 1969.

*Herskovits, Melville J. *The Myth of the Negro Past.* 2nd ed. Boston, 1958.

*Horrabin, J. F. *An Atlas of Africa.* New York, 1960.

*July, Robert W. *A History of the African People.* New York, 1970.

*Oliver, Roland and J. D. Fage. *A Short History of Africa.* Harmondsworth, England, 1962.

B. West Africa in Early Times

The Art of Western Africa: Sculpture and Tribal Masks. Introduction by William Fagg. New York, 1967.

Bovill, E. W. *The Golden Trade of the Moors.* 2nd ed. London, 1968.

*De Graft-Johnson, John C. *African Glory; the Story of Vanished Negro Civilizations.* New York, 1955.

*Shinnie, Margaret. *Ancient African Kimgdoms.* London, 1965.

C. The European Impact: Slave Trading and the Era of Exploration and Imperialism

Curtin, Philip D. *The African Slave Trade: A Census.* Madison, 1969.

234

*Davidson, Basil. *Black Mother: The Years of the African Slave Trade.* London, 1961.

*Duffy, James. *Portugal in Africa.* Harmondsworth, England, 1962.

*Fyfe, Christopher. *A Short History of Sierra Leone.* 6th ed. London, 1969.

*Liebenow, J. Gus. *Liberia: The Evolution of Privilege.* Ithaca, 1969.

*Mannix, Daniel P. and Malcolm Cowley. *Black Cargoes: A History of the Atlantic Slave Trade, 1518–1865.* New York, 1962.

*Perham, Margery and J. Simmons, eds. *African Discovery: An Anthology of Exploration.* 2nd ed. London, 1957.

*Robinson, Ronald, John Gallagher and Alice Denny. *Africa and the Victorians.* New York, 1961.

*Tannenbaum, Frank. *Slave and Citizen: The Negro in the Americas.* New York, 1946.

D. *The Colonial Reckoning: The Rise of Nationalism and the Coming of Independence*

*Achebe, Chinua. *Things Fall Apart.* New York, 1969.

*———. *No Longer At Ease.* New York, 1969.

*Adloff, Richard. *West Africa: The French-Speaking Nations.* New York, 1964.

*Armah, Ayi Kwei. *The Beautyful Ones Are Not Yet Born.* New York, 1968.

*Carty, Wilfred and Martin Kilson, eds. *The Africa Reader.* 2 vols. New York, 1970.

*Ekwensi, Cyprian. *People of the City.* New York, 1954.

*———. *Jagua Nana.* New York, 1961.

*Hargreaves, John D. *West Africa: The Former French States.* Englewood Cliffs, 1967.

*Hatch, John. *A History of Postwar Africa.* New York, 1965.

*Hodgkin, Thomas. *Nationalism in Colonial Africa.* London, 1956.

*Legum, Colin. *Pan-Africanism: A Short Political Guide.* Rev. ed. New York, 1965.

*Nkrumah, Kwame. *Ghana: the Autobiography of Kwame Nkrumah.* London, 1957.

Nwankwo, Arthur A. and Samuel U. Ifejika. *Biafra: The Making of a Nation.* New York, 1969.

*Post, Ken. *The New States of West Africa.* Harmondsworth, England, 1964.

*Reed, J. and C. Wake. *A Book of African Verse.* London, 1964.

*Wallbank, T. Walter. *Documents on Modern Africa.* Princeton, 1964.

*Wallerstein, Immanuel. *Africa: The Politics of Independence.* New York, 1961.

INDEX

Abeokuta, 44, 66, 67, 115, 162
abolition, *see* anti-slavery movement *and* slave trade
Abomey, 62, 63, 67
Aborigines Rights' Protection Society, 172
Abu Bakr, 7, 8
Achebe, Chinua, xi, xii
Accra, 54, 61, 83, 122, 173, 200
Action Group of Western Nigeria, 181
Adams, Capt. John, on Old Calabar, 79
Adandozan, 65
Addis Ababa, conference at, 198, 204
African Association, 110, 131, 145 – 47
African Orthodox Church, 175
Africanus, Leo, quotes from, 14, 17, 18, 22, 33, 36
Agaja, 62, 63, 64
Agonglo, 65
Aguiyi-Ironsi, General J. T. U., 193, 209
Ahidjo, Ahmadou, 211
Ahmad, of Kanem-Bornu, 27
Ahmadu II, 73
Ahmadu Séku, 74, 160
Ahmed el-Mansur, 19
Aja, 62
Akaba, 62
Akan, origins of, 51
Akassa, 78, 83
Akim, and Akwamu, 54
Akintola, Samuel, 192, 193, 208, 209
Akufo-Addo, Edward, 207
Akwamu, 52, 53, 54
Ali, of Kanem-Bornu, 24, 25
Ali Ghaji, 23
Aliu Baba, 73, 75
All-African Peoples Conference, 200
All People's Congress, 124, 125
Allada, Dahomey and, 42, 62, 63
Alley, Alphonse, 212
Almoravides, 7, 69
Aluewu, 43
America, slave markets in, 77; *see also* North America *and* United States
American Colonization Society, 128 – 33

American Firestone Company, 139, 141
American Revolution, slaves and, 109, 112
Americo-Liberians, 136 – 38, 141 – 42
Ancient Ghana, xiii, 3 – 8, 69; *see also* Ghana
Ankrah, General Joseph, 207
anti-slavery movement, 94 – 103, 115, 146, 149 – 50
Apithy, Sourou-Migan, 212, 214
Aqua, King, 80
Arguin Island, 86, 89
Ashanti, xiii, 50 – 61, 90; and Mossi, 30, 31, 53; birth of, 51, 52; and Denkyira, 51 – 3; expansion of, 53 – 5; and Fanti, 54 – 9, 170; and British, 55 – 61, 119, 162, 170; and independence, 60; and Gold Coast, 61, 162; resistance by, 162; *see also* Dahomey *and* slave trade
Ashmun, Jehudi, 131 – 2
Askia Ishak, and Moroccans, 19
Askia Muhammad, 17, 18
Askia Musa, 18
Atiku, 73
Attahiru, 75 – 76
Audoghast, 4, 7
Awolowo, Obafemi, 181, 192, 208
Axim, Dutch and, 89, 92
Azikiwe, Nnamdi, 170, 180 – 82

Badagry, 64, 66
Bakary, Djibo, 220
Bakri, El, 5, 6, 7
Balewa, Abubakar Tafawa, 182, 193, 209
Bamaka, conference at, 184, 188
Barclay, Edwin, 140, 142
Barreiro, on Sierra Leone, 107
Barth, Heinrich, 150 – 1; quotes from, 32, 34, 36
Bawo, Prince, 32
Beecroft, John, 80, 83, 150
Behanzin, 67, 160
Behn, Mrs. Aphra, 94
Belgium, 152, 157, 158
Bello, Sir Ahmadu, 181, 182, 192, 193, 209
Bello, Muhammad, 72 – 4; quotes from, 35, 36, 38, 69
Benin, 39, 44 – 50, 86, 162; art of, xiii, 44, 47 – 8; and Yoruba, 38; description of, 44 – 6; origins of,

237